KOS TRAVEL GUIDE

2025

Your Comprehensive Companion to Explore Greek Island Paradise: Discover the Beauty and Natural Wonders

Christy T Davis

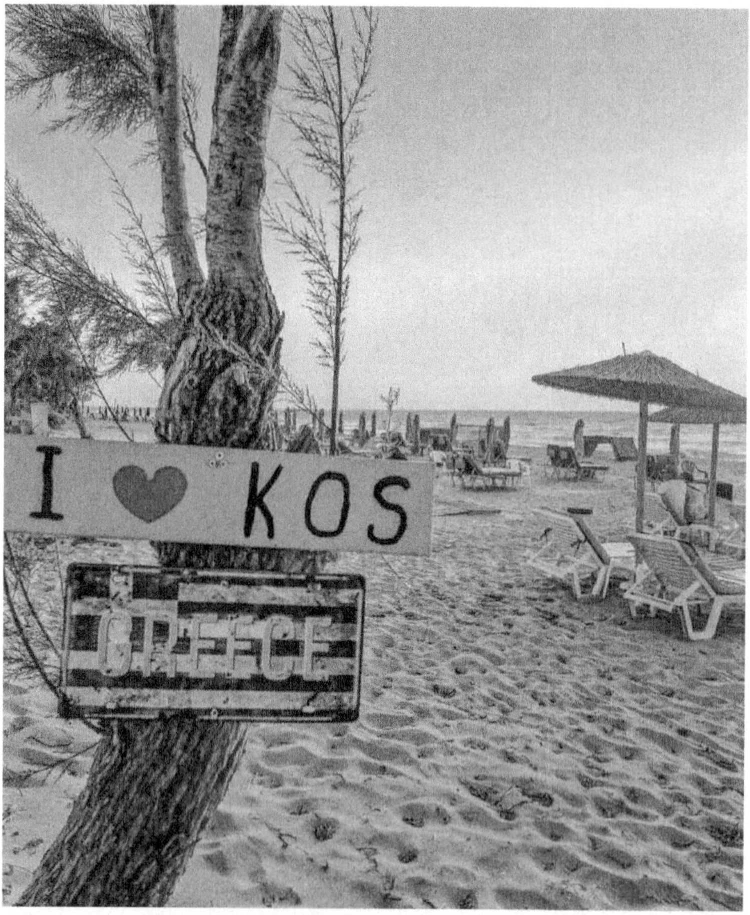
I KOS
GREECE

Copyright © [2024] by [Christy T. Davis].

All rights reserved. No part of this publication may be reproduced, distributed, or transmitted in any form or by any means, including photocopying, recording, or other electronic or mechanical methods, without the prior written permission of the publisher, except in the case of brief quotations embodied in critical reviews and certain other noncommercial uses permitted by copyright law.

Table of contents

Chapter 1. Introduction to Kos Island
- Overview of Kos
- Historical Significance
- Geography and Landscape
- Best Time to Visit
- Why Visit Kos Island

Chapter 2. Getting to Kos Island
- International and Domestic Flights
- Ferry Services
- Local Transportation Options

Map

Chapter 3. Accommodation on Kos Island
- Luxury Hotels and Resorts
- Budget-Friendly Options
- Beachfront Villas
- Hostels and Guesthouses

Chapter 4. Top Attractions in Kos
- Asklepion of Kos
- Ancient Agora
- Tree of Hippocrates
- Roman Odeon

- Neratzia Castle
- Zia Village
- Thermes Hot Springs

Chapter 5. Kos Island Towns and Villages
- Kos Town
- Kardamena
- Kefalos
- Tigaki
- Mastichari
- Antimachia
- Pyli

Chapter 6. Outdoor Activities and Nature
- Hiking and Nature Trails
- Water Sports and Diving
- Cycling Routes
- Guided Tours and Excursions

Chapter 7. Food and Drink on Kos Island
- Traditional Kos Cuisine
- Best Local Restaurants
- Local Markets and Street Food
- Wine and Olive Oil Tasting

Chapter 8. Culture and Traditions
- Festivals and Celebrations
- Local Crafts and Souvenirs

- Music and Dance

- Kos Folklore and Myths

Chapter 9. Practical Information

- Health and Safety Tips

- Currency, Banking, and ATMs

- Communication and Language

- Travel Insurance and Emergency Contacts

Chapter 10. Day Trips and Nearby Islands

- Nisyros Island

- Kalymnos Island

- Pserimos Island

- Plati Island

- Patmos Island

Chapter 11. A Perfect 3 Days Itinerary

Conclusion

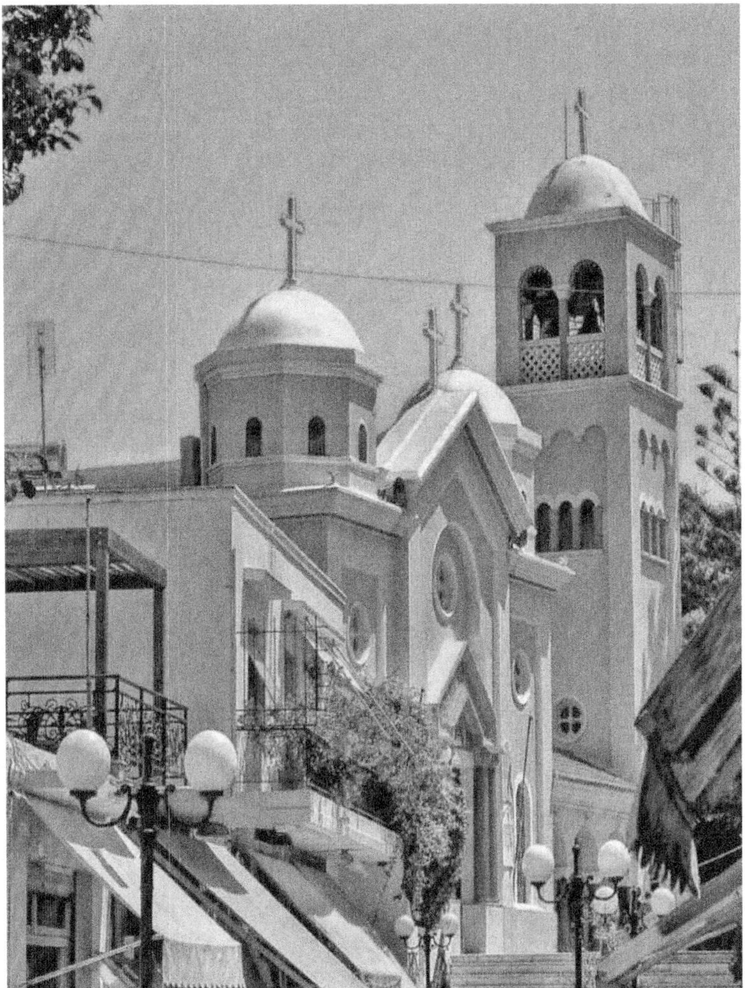

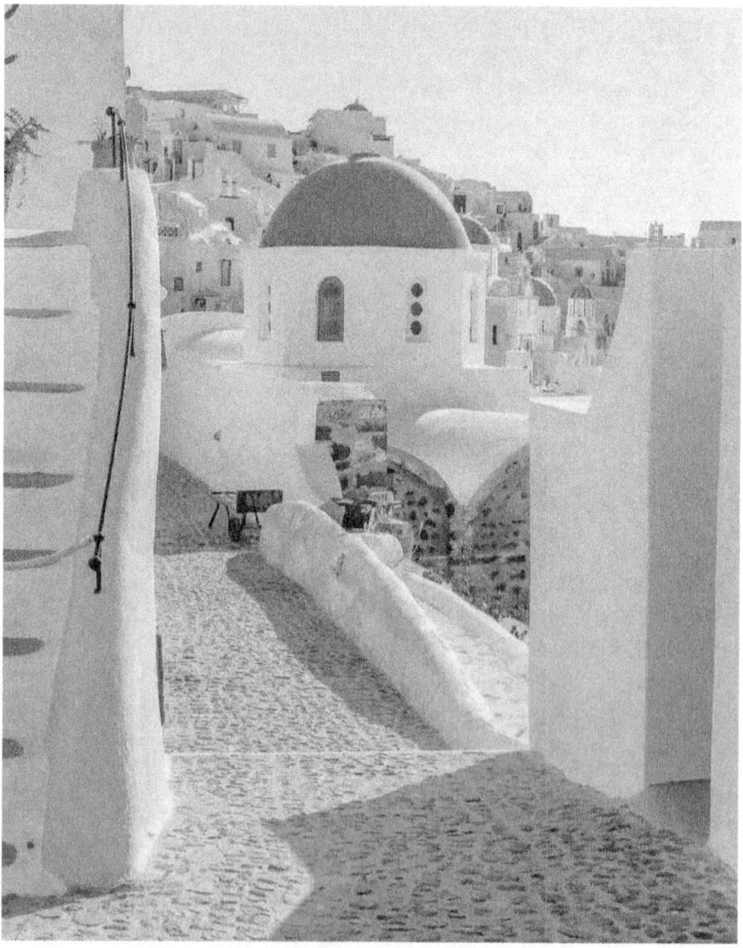

Chapter 1. Introduction to Kos Island

- Overview of Kos

Kos, the third largest island in the Dodecanese group, is a beloved destination for travelers. Families, friends, and couples flock to its vibrant nightlife, savor local cuisine, engage in various activities, and enjoy comfortable accommodations. The island offers everything one could wish for: hospitable locals, stunning beaches, picturesque villages, and numerous historic sites to explore. Known as the home of Hippocrates, the father of medicine, Kos feels like an open-air museum, showcasing ancient and medieval monuments, archaeological sites, and buildings from the Italian Rule. Inhabited since ancient times, the island has been shaped by a multitude of foreign cultures over the centuries. Exploring Kos by bike allows you to discover both the town and smaller villages, each filled with monuments that tell the island's rich history. It's a destination that caters to all ages and tastes, especially those who love outdoor activities in nature!

- Historical Significance

In Greek mythology, Kos is the holy region of Asclepius, the god of healing. Archaeological studies show that Kos' history began in ancient periods, with some remnants recovered going back to the Bronze Age (2900 BC-2100 BC). The Minoans arrived on the island in the 14th century BC, followed by the Achaeans and, a few years later, the Dorians, who founded the ancient city of Kos. The Persians occupied Kos in the fifth century BC, but were defeated by the Athenians, who seized possession of the island after the Battle of Salamina.

The fifth century BC saw the birth of Hippocrates, the father of medicine and the founder of the first School of Medicine. After his death in 357 BC, the people of Kos constructed the Asklepeion shrine, which honors

Hippocrates and the deity Asklepios. It served as a hospital, accepting patients from all around the Mediterranean and employing physicians who employed Hippocrates' medicinal techniques.

During the Peloponnesian War between Athens and Sparta (431 BC-404 BC), the inhabitants of Kos were allies of Athens but switched sides based on their interests. In 394 BC, Kos renewed its alliance with Athens, and democracy was brought to the island. This time period saw significant cultural, educational, and economic advancement.

The Macedonian Empire incorporated the island of Kos in 335 BC. Following Alexander the Great's death, his successors, the Ptolemies, gained control of the island and the remainder of the Dodecanese. The Byzantine era brought prosperity and luxury to Kos, but it was endangered by regular pirate incursions, the most deadly of which were Saracen invasions.

After 82 BC, Kos became part of the Roman Empire's Eastern colony. The Venetians seized the island in 1204 AD, and the Knights of Saint John claimed sovereignty in 1315. A century later, they erected the magnificent castle that still stands at the entrance to Kos' port, as well as the Castle of Antimachia. The Turks took over the island in 1522 and remained there until 1912, when Italian troops invaded and evicted them. The Italians saw the island as a major tourist destination and were in charge of a number of infrastructural improvements and archeological explorations.

Following the terrible earthquake of 1934, which almost devastated Kos and damaged many buildings, infrastructure renovations were a top priority. The Italians' control ended in 1943, when German soldiers invaded the island. The German occupation was a sad era for the people of Kos, who suffered much. The horror came to an end in 1945, when Kos was placed under British administration. Finally, the Paris Peace Treaty reunited Kos and the remainder of the Dodecanese with Greece in 1948.

Since then, Kos has grown at a rapid rate and taken its own path. After the 1980s, a large number of visitors began to visit Kos, and the island's infrastructure and services developed dramatically. Kos has become one of the world's most popular travel destinations.

- Geography and Landscape

Kos is the third largest island in the Dodecanese group, after Rhodes and Karpathos. It is located south of Kalymnos and north of Nisyros, along Turkey's coastlines and around 200 nautical miles from Piraeus. This geographic place has a rich local history that dates back to prehistoric times. The island has a total size of 290 square kilometers, a shoreline of 112 kilometers, and a population of more than 35,000.

The Kos mainland is lush and productive, with good soil and plenty of groundwater. The island is primarily flat, with two minor mountains. Mount Dikaion is the tallest, standing at 846 meters, and Mount Simpatro extends along Kos' southern coast. Kos also has several breathtaking natural structures, such as the Cave of Aspri Petra, also known as the Cave of the White Stone, located on Mount Zini.

The Forest of Plaka is a large pine forest near the village of Antimachia that represents the island's rich vegetation and picturesque natural environs. The Alyki Wetland, located between the villages of Marmari and Tigaki, is a natural environment for a diverse range of flora and wildlife and is protected under Natura 2000. The Psalidi Wetland is another important natural habitat for a variety of animal species.

Kos Town, the island's capital and primary harbor, is located in a lush region. The settlement is located in the northeastern portion of the island, overlooking a natural harbor (an open bay). One of the town's features is the Hippocrates Tree in Platanos Square, which is considered one of Europe's oldest trees. There are open thermal springs, or thermes, near the town that contain hot volcanic water.

Kos' landscape is marked by its massive 112-kilometer-long coastline dotted with golden beaches. Some of the most popular beaches include Mastichari Beach, which has an exotic atmosphere and green waters, Marmari Beach, which has white sand, and Paradise Beach. Many magnificent islets lie directly opposite the island's shore, such as the picturesque Kastri Islet beside Kefalos Beach.

Climate

Kos enjoys a Mediterranean climate, with hot, dry summers and mild, wet winters. This climate is perfect for both agriculture and tourism, making Kos a year-round destination.

- Best Time to Visit

Kos, a beautiful Greek island, is well-known for its stunning beaches, lush valleys, and rich history. It is part of the Dodecanese island group in the southeastern Aegean Sea and provides an unforgettable holiday experience for visitors from all over the world. The best time to visit this picturesque island can make a big difference in one's experience, as the weather and tourist crowds influence the overall atmosphere.

For most visitors, the best time to plan a trip to Kos is between late May and early October, when the weather is consistently warm and sunny, ideal for lazy days on the beach. During these months, visitors can enjoy comfortable temperatures, warm azure waters, and a lively atmosphere. However, it is important to note that these peak months can bring larger crowds and a thriving tourist scene.

To avoid the peak season and have a more relaxing vacation, consider visiting Kos during the milder spring and autumn months, when temperatures average around 23°C and rainfall is rare. This off-peak period allows you to explore the island's treasures at a slower pace while still enjoying the beautiful weather and scenery that make Kos such a popular holiday destination.

Spring

Spring is a great time to visit Kos, particularly between late May and early June. During this time, the weather is generally warm and sunny, ideal for relaxing beach days. Furthermore, the island is less crowded, allowing visitors to enjoy a more relaxing atmosphere. Here's a quick overview of the average spring temperatures:
- April: 11°C (low) – 20°C (high)
- May: 15°C (low) – 25°C (high)
- June: 19°C (low) – 29°C (high)

Some benefits of visiting Kos in the spring include:
- Good weather for sightseeing.
- Less crowded tourist attractions and beaches.
- Reasonable accommodation prices.

Autumn

Autumn is also an excellent time to visit Kos, especially from September to early October. During these months, the weather remains warm, and the number of tourists

begins to decline following the busy summer season. Here are the average autumn temperatures:
- September: 19°C (low) – 28°C (high)
- October: 15°C (low) – 24°C (high)
- November: 11°C (low) – 19°C (high)
-

The advantages of visiting Kos in autumn include:
- Suitable weather for outdoor activities.
- Less crowded attractions and beaches than in summer.
- Competitive accommodation prices

Spring and autumn visitors can expect warmer daytime temperatures and cooler evenings. Pack light layers, sunscreen, and comfortable shoes to fully enjoy the stunning island of Kos while avoiding the peak summer crowds.

Weather Overview

Temperature

Kos, a picturesque Greek island, enjoys a Mediterranean climate characterized by warm summers and mild winters. From late May to early October, the weather is consistently warm and sunny, making it ideal for relaxing days at the beach. August has the highest temperatures, often reaching 29°C and rarely dropping below 21°C.

However, winter is the island's coldest season, with temperatures as low as 15.4°C in January. This month's average temperature is approximately 11.2°C, with a minimum of 8.9°C and a maximum of 13.6°C. On the coldest nights, the temperature may drop as low as 3.5°C. During the winter months, sea temperatures range between 16 and 18 degrees Celsius, making it too cold for most people to swim.

Precipitation

While Kos has mostly warm and sunny weather during the summer, there are occasional periods of rain and precipitation. The wettest season is winter, with the highest average rainfall of 120mm in January. If you plan to visit Kos during the winter, be prepared to wrap up and bring an umbrella, as rain is more likely during this time of year.

In contrast, the summer months are relatively dry, with significantly less precipitation. This makes the period between late May and early October a popular time to visit the island, as visitors can enjoy nice weather and spend time outside without having to deal with frequent rain.

What to pack?

When planning a trip to Kos, it is critical to consider what to bring in order to have a comfortable and enjoyable stay. Here are some specific clothing and essential items to pack for your trip to the Greek island of Kos.

Clothing

Lightweight and breathable clothing: Because Kos has a hot Mediterranean climate, particularly during the summer months, it is best to pack lightweight, breathable clothing like cotton T-shirts, shorts, skirts, and dresses.

Swimwear: With its beautiful beaches and warm waters, swimming and water activities are popular in Kos. Make sure you bring enough swimwear for the duration of your stay.

Sun protection: Bring a wide-brimmed hat and sunglasses. Also, bring light cover-ups or shawls to protect your shoulders from the sun while exploring the island.

Comfortable walking shoes: Exploring the island may require walking on uneven surfaces. For your adventures around Kos, pack comfortable walking shoes, such as sneakers or sandals with good arch support.

A light jacket or cardigan: Although Kos is known for its warm weather, evenings can be cool. A light jacket or cardigan is ideal for evening strolls or outdoor dinners.

Essential Items

Sunscreen: The sun can be harsh in Kos, particularly during the summer months. Make sure to bring a high SPF sunscreen (30 or higher) and reapply it throughout the day to protect your skin.

Insect repellent: Mosquitoes are common on the island, so bring insect repellent to avoid bites.

Reusable water bottle: Staying hydrated in the hot sun is essential. Bring a reusable water bottle with you and refill it as needed during the day.

Travel adaptor: Greece uses a different type of plug than most other countries. Pack a universal travel adaptor so you can charge your electronic devices.

A small first aid kit containing essentials such as pain relievers, plasters, and any personal medications is always useful to keep on hand during your trip.

- Why Visit Kos Island

Kos is undeniably one of the gems of the southeastern Mediterranean. Each year, around 2.5 million visitors arrive to uncover the island's many wonders. Some come for the relaxing, all-inclusive experience of popular Kardamena in the south, while others are drawn to the stylish atmosphere of Kamari. Many choose to retreat to the charming mountain villages nestled in the Dikeos range, while some prefer the lively energy of Kos Town, known for its vibrant nightlife.

1. Beautiful Beaches

Kos is renowned for its magnificent beaches with crystal-clear waters. Whether you prefer bustling beaches with plenty of amenities like Tigaki and Kardamena, or more secluded spots like Cavo Paradiso, there's a perfect beach for everyone.

2. Rich History and Archaeological Sites

Kos is steeped in history, with numerous archaeological sites to explore. Visit the Asklepieion, an ancient healing temple, the Roman Odeon, and the medieval Castle of the Knights of Saint John. The island's historical richness offers a fascinating journey through time.

3. Delicious Greek Cuisine

The island's gastronomy is a delightful blend of Greek, Italian, and Turkish influences. Enjoy fresh seafood, local cheeses, and traditional dishes like moussaka and souvlaki. Dining in Kos is a treat for the senses, with many tavernas offering stunning sea views.

4. Vibrant Nightlife

Kos boasts a lively nightlife scene, especially in Kos Town and Kardamena. From beach bars and nightclubs to more relaxed cocktail lounges, there's something for everyone. The island comes alive after dark, offering endless entertainment options.

5. Picturesque Villages and Natural Beauty

Explore the charming villages of Kos, such as Zia and Kefalos, which offer stunning views and a glimpse into traditional Greek life. The island's natural beauty is also evident in its lush landscapes, hot springs, and serene forests.

Kos Island truly has something for everyone, making it a must-visit destination!

Chapter 2. Getting to Kos Island

- International and Domestic Flights

Kos, a beautiful Greek island in the Dodecanese, offers stunning beaches, lush valleys, and a rich history. When planning a visit to Kos, there are limited ways to get there, depending on your starting point. However, you essentially have only two options: you can either fly or sail to the island.

International Flights

Kos Island International Airport, also known as "Hippocrates" Airport (IATA code: KGS), receives numerous international flights, especially during the peak tourist season from April to October. Many airlines, including Ryanair, easyJet, Eurowings, Jet2, Condor, and TUI Fly, offer direct flights to Kos from various

European cities such as London, Manchester, Berlin, Amsterdam, and Zurich. The longest direct flight to Kos is from Glasgow, taking around 4 hours and 45 minutes. Additionally, airlines from countries like the UK, Germany, Italy, France, and the Netherlands operate charter and low-cost flights to Kos, providing a convenient option for travelers seeking a beach holiday. Some major European cities also have year-round flights, allowing for easy access even outside the summer months.

Domestic Flights

If you're traveling within Greece, the most common route to Kos is through Athens. Aegean Airlines and Sky Express offer frequent flights from Athens International Airport (Eleftherios Venizelos) to Kos, with a flight duration of about one hour. Kos is well-connected through domestic flights, providing excellent connections for those visiting other Greek islands or exploring the mainland. During the summer, there are also flights to and from Thessaloniki and other islands like Rhodes and Crete, further enhancing the accessibility of Kos.

- Ferry Services

Kos Island is easily accessible by ferry, making it a popular option for travelers seeking to explore the Greek islands by sea. Kos is part of the Dodecanese group, and its strategic location allows it to be well-connected to other islands and mainland Greece through regular ferry services.

Ferries from Mainland Greece

The main port connecting Kos to the mainland is Piraeus Port in Athens. Several ferry companies, including Blue Star Ferries and Dodekanisos Seaways, operate routes between Piraeus and Kos. The ferry journey from Piraeus to Kos typically takes around 8 to 12 hours, depending on the type of vessel and the number of stops along the way. Overnight ferries are available, allowing travelers to arrive in Kos refreshed and ready to explore.

Ferries from Other Greek Islands

Kos is also connected to several other Greek islands, making it a perfect hub for island hopping. Frequent ferries run between Kos and nearby islands like Rhodes, Kalymnos, Nisyros, Patmos, and Leros. Additionally, there are ferry services to Crete and Santorini during the peak summer months, providing further opportunities to explore the beauty of the Greek islands. High-speed ferries, which are faster but more expensive, are also available on certain routes.

International Ferry Connections

For travelers coming from Turkey, Kos has a direct ferry connection to the Turkish town of Bodrum, located just 20 kilometers across the sea. The journey from Bodrum to Kos takes about 45 minutes to 1 hour, making it an easy and popular day trip for visitors from both countries. Several operators run daily routes during the summer season.

- Local Transportation Options

Kos Island offers a variety of transportation options, making it easy to explore its many attractions, beaches, and villages. From public buses to rental services, visitors can choose the most convenient mode of transport based on their preferences and itinerary.

Public Buses

Public buses are a convenient and affordable way to travel around Kos. The bus service is operated by KTEL, and there are two main types of buses: island buses and city buses.

- **Island Buses:** These buses connect Kos Town to the airport and major beach resorts such as Tigaki, Marmari, Kefalos, Mastichari, and Kardamena. They run regularly throughout the day, especially during the tourist season. The main KTEL bus station is located behind the old town, about a 10-minute walk from the harbor.

Tickets can be purchased on the bus or from the assistant as you board.

- **City Buses:** These buses operate within Kos Town and its immediate surroundings, including areas like Psalidi, Agios Fokas, Lambi, Alikarnassos, and Platani. Tickets for city buses must be bought before boarding, available at the small waterfront bus station south of the harbor and castle

Taxis

Taxis are available across Kos Island, with taxi ranks located in key areas such as Kos Town, Kardamena, and Mastichari. They are a more expensive option than buses but offer the convenience of door-to-door service, especially when traveling with luggage or in a group. Taxis can be flagged down on the street, or arrangements can be made by phone for scheduled pick-ups. While taxi meters are used for most trips, it's common to agree on a fixed price for longer journeys. Rates are reasonable, and tipping is not obligatory but appreciated.

Car Rentals

Renting a car is a popular option for those wanting the freedom to explore Kos at their own pace. Several car rental agencies operate at Kos International Airport, in Kos Town, and in popular tourist areas like Kardamena and Kefalos. Options range from small economy cars to larger family vehicles and even SUVs for off-road adventures. Renting a car allows easy access to more remote beaches, mountain villages, and archaeological sites that may not be served by public transport. It's important to note that during the high season, booking a rental car in advance is advisable to secure the best rates and availability.

Scooter, ATV, and Bicycle Rentals

For a more adventurous way to explore the island, scooters, ATVs, and bicycles are widely available for rent. Scooters and ATVs are a great way to navigate narrow village roads and coastal paths, offering the flexibility to park easily in crowded areas. They are ideal for those looking to explore off-the-beaten-path spots or make quick trips between beaches. Helmets are mandatory for both scooters and ATVs. Bicycle rentals are also popular, especially in Kos Town, where bike lanes make cycling a safe and enjoyable option. The flat terrain of the island's north coast makes biking an excellent choice for those looking to combine exercise with sightseeing.

Boat Rentals and Water Taxis

For travelers interested in exploring Kos from the water, boat rentals and water taxis offer a unique perspective. Small boats and yachts can be rented at Kos Marina or from other coastal towns, allowing for private trips around the island or visits to nearby islets like Pserimos and Kalymnos. Water taxis also operate between Kos Town and surrounding beaches or smaller harbors. This can be a relaxing and scenic way to access remote beaches or spend a day at sea.

Private Transfers and Tours

Private transfer services are available for those who prefer the convenience of personalized transportation. These can be arranged for airport pick-ups, hotel transfers, or custom island tours. Private vehicles, often with English-speaking drivers, offer a comfortable and flexible way to explore the island without the need to navigate public transportation schedules or drive. Many local companies also offer guided tours to historical sites, beaches, and wineries, combining transportation with an informative experience.

Walking

Kos Island is also a pedestrian-friendly destination, particularly in Kos Town, where many attractions, shops, and restaurants are within walking distance. The town features well-maintained sidewalks, pedestrian zones, and waterfront promenades that are ideal for leisurely strolls. Walking is especially enjoyable in the evening when the town's historic buildings and harbor are beautifully illuminated.

Each transportation option in Kos offers unique advantages, allowing visitors to tailor their travel experience according to their interests and needs.

Map

Scan the above QR code for your map

Chapter 3. Accommodation on Kos Island

- Luxury Hotels and Resorts

1. Blue Pearls - Adults Only Luxury Suites (Kos Town)

Blue Pearls offers an exclusive, adults-only experience with luxurious suites designed for ultimate comfort and relaxation. Each suite features modern decor, a private terrace, and stunning sea views. The property boasts an infinity pool overlooking the Aegean Sea, a lush garden, and a stylish bar. Guests can enjoy direct beach access, complimentary Wi-Fi, and free parking. The location is perfect for exploring nearby attractions like the Asclepieion of Kos and Kos Port, making it an ideal choice for a tranquil getaway.

2. OKU Kos (Marmari)

OKU Kos is a village-style, adults-only hotel situated on a pristine sandy beach. The resort offers spacious rooms and suites with minimalist design, private terraces, and some with private pools. The on-site restaurant serves a variety of Mediterranean dishes made from locally sourced ingredients. Guests can unwind at the luxurious spa, which includes an indoor pool, hammam, and a range of treatments. The outdoor pool area is surrounded by well-tended gardens, providing a serene environment for relaxation. The fitness center and yoga classes cater to those looking to stay active during their stay.

3. D' Andrea Lagoon All Suites - Adults Only (Marmari)

This chic, adults-only hotel in Marmari offers a serene retreat with luxurious suites featuring contemporary decor and private balconies. The property includes a gourmet restaurant serving international cuisine, a stylish bar, and a shared lounge area. Guests can enjoy the large outdoor pool, surrounded by sun loungers and cabanas, perfect for soaking up the sun. The hotel also offers room service, concierge services, and free private parking, ensuring a comfortable and hassle-free stay.

4. Theros All Suite Hotel - Adults Only (Kos Town)

Theros All Suite Hotel provides a sophisticated and luxurious ambiance, perfect for adults seeking a high-end experience. The beachfront hotel features elegantly designed suites with private balconies or terraces, offering stunning sea views. The seasonal outdoor swimming pool is complemented by a well-equipped fitness center and a beautifully landscaped garden. Guests can relax at the private beach area or enjoy a drink at the stylish bar. The hotel also offers a terrace for dining and lounging, making it an ideal spot for a romantic getaway.

5. Albergo Gelsomino (Kos Town)

Albergo Gelsomino is a historic, Italian-inspired boutique hotel offering elegant accommodations with a touch of old-world charm. The 5-star hotel features beautifully appointed rooms with high ceilings, classic furnishings, and modern amenities. The shared lounge and terrace provide comfortable spaces for relaxation, while the on-site restaurant serves exquisite Mediterranean cuisine. Located right on the beachfront, guests can enjoy easy access to the sea and stunning views of the harbor. The hotel's stylish design and prime location make it a standout choice for luxury travelers.

6. NISSEA Boutique Hotel (Kardamaina)

NISSEA Boutique Hotel, located in the vibrant area of Kardamaina, offers charming and elegant accommodations with a cozy atmosphere. The 5-star boutique hotel features tastefully decorated rooms with private balconies, some offering sea views. The property includes a bar, a garden, and a terrace where guests can unwind and enjoy the serene surroundings. The hotel's central location provides easy access to local attractions, shops, and restaurants, making it a convenient base for exploring the island. The intimate setting and personalized service make NISSEA a popular choice for those seeking a luxurious and intimate stay.

- Budget-Friendly Options

1. Hotel Sonia (Kos Town)

Hotel Sonia offers a cozy and budget-friendly stay in the heart of Kos Town. The rooms are clean and comfortable, equipped with basic amenities such as air conditioning, a refrigerator, and free Wi-Fi. The hotel is within walking distance of the beach, local shops, and restaurants, making it a convenient base for exploring the town. The friendly staff are always ready to assist with any needs, ensuring a pleasant stay.
- Price: Approximately $50 per night.

2. Captain's Hotel (Kos Town)

Captain's Hotel provides affordable accommodations with a central location in Kos Town. The hotel features a refreshing swimming pool, a bar, and a breakfast area where guests can start their day. The rooms are simple yet comfortable, equipped with air conditioning, a TV, and free Wi-Fi. The hotel is close to the harbor, making it easy to explore the town and its attractions.
- Price: Approximately $45 per night.

3. Fantasia Hotel Apartments (Kos Town)

Fantasia Hotel Apartments offers spacious and budget-friendly accommodations ideal for longer stays. Each apartment includes a kitchenette, allowing guests to prepare their own meals. The rooms are equipped with air conditioning, a TV, and free Wi-Fi. The hotel is located near the beach and within walking distance of various shops and restaurants, providing convenience and comfort.

- Price: Approximately $40 per night.

4. Olympia Hotel (Kos Town)

Olympia Hotel is a budget-friendly option that provides a welcoming atmosphere and comfortable accommodations. The hotel features a charming garden and a terrace where guests can relax. Rooms are equipped with air conditioning, a TV, and free Wi-Fi. The hotel is conveniently located near the center of Kos Town, offering easy access to the harbor, shops, and restaurants.

- Price: Approximately $35 per night.

5. Hotel Koala (Kos Town)

Hotel Koala is a family-run hotel that offers affordable rates and a cozy environment. The hotel features a swimming pool, a bar, and a breakfast area. Rooms are equipped with air conditioning, a TV, and free Wi-Fi. The hotel is within walking distance of the beach and Kos Town's main attractions, making it a great choice for budget-conscious travelers.

- Price: Approximately $40 per night.

These budget-friendly options provide comfortable and convenient accommodations without breaking the bank, making them perfect for travelers looking to explore Kos on a budget.

- Beachfront Villas

1. TAF Boutique Beachfront Villas (Tigaki)

TAF Boutique Beachfront Villas offer an exquisite beachfront experience with luxurious amenities. Each villa features a private heated pool, perfect for a relaxing

swim any time of the year. The villas are elegantly designed with modern interiors and spacious living areas. Guests can enjoy the convenience of a Tesla Model Y for eco-friendly travel around the island. Daily housekeeping services ensure that the villas are always in pristine condition. The location in Tigaki provides easy access to beautiful beaches and local attractions.
- Price: Approximately $200 per night.

2. DS Luxury House (Kardamena)

DS Luxury House is a stunning beachfront villa located in Kardamena. The villa boasts an outdoor swimming pool, a beautifully landscaped garden, and a terrace with breathtaking sea views. Inside, the villa features two spacious bedrooms, a fully equipped kitchen, and modern amenities such as free Wi-Fi and air conditioning. The stylish decor and comfortable furnishings make it an ideal choice for a luxurious getaway. The villa's proximity to the beach allows guests to enjoy the sun and sea with ease.
- Price: Approximately $250 per night.

3. Villa Kos (Mastichari)

Villa Kos offers a serene beachfront retreat just 300 meters from a sandy beach and close to Lido Water Park. The villa includes a large terrace where guests can relax and enjoy the sea breeze. The interior is modern and well-appointed, with a fully equipped kitchen, comfortable living spaces, and free Wi-Fi. The villa is perfect for families or groups looking for a peaceful holiday by the sea. The nearby attractions and amenities make it a convenient and enjoyable place to stay.

- Price: Approximately $350 per night.

4. Alta Vista Luxury House (Kardamena)

Alta Vista Luxury House provides a luxurious stay with stunning mountain and sea views. The villa features two elegantly decorated bedrooms, a fully equipped kitchen, and a hot tub for ultimate relaxation. Guests can enjoy the spacious balcony and terrace, perfect for dining al fresco or simply taking in the beautiful surroundings. The villa also offers free Wi-Fi and private parking. Its location in Kardamena provides easy access to local shops, restaurants, and the beach.

- Price: Approximately $450 per night.

5. Phillyrèa Luxury Villas (Kos Town)

Phillyrèa Luxury Villas offer an exceptional beachfront experience with an infinity pool and panoramic sea views. Each villa is designed with modern elegance, featuring air conditioning, a fully equipped kitchen, and a flat-screen TV. The spacious living areas and private terraces provide the perfect setting for relaxation and entertainment. Guests can enjoy the convenience of private parking and easy access to the vibrant Kos Town, with its array of shops, restaurants, and historical sites.
- Price: Approximately $280 per night.

These beachfront villas provide luxurious amenities, stunning views, and convenient locations, ensuring a memorable and indulgent stay on Kos Island.

- Hostels and Guesthouses

1. Leonidas Hotel and Studios (Kos Town)

Leonidas Hotel and Studios is a family-run establishment located just 800 meters from the nearest sandy beach and 900 meters from the bustling center of Kos Town. The hotel offers a quiet location with easy access to the island's main attractions. Rooms are equipped with air conditioning, a refrigerator, and free Wi-Fi. Guests can enjoy the outdoor swimming pool, sun terrace, and a bar. The friendly staff and comfortable accommodations make it a great budget-friendly option.
- Price: Approximately $30 per night.

2. Alexandra Hotel & Apartments (Kos Town)

Alexandra Hotel & Apartments provides a budget-friendly setting with a mix of comfort and convenience. Located in the heart of Kos Town, the hotel offers air-conditioned rooms with a refrigerator and free Wi-Fi. Guests have access to a 24-hour front desk, room service, and express check-in and check-out. The hotel also features a swimming pool, a lounge, and free public

parking nearby. Its central location makes it easy to explore the town's attractions.
- Price: Approximately $35 per night.

3. Kos Bay Hotel (Kos Town)

Kos Bay Hotel is an excellent choice for budget travelers, offering a friendly environment and helpful amenities. The hotel is located close to top attractions like Hippocrates Tree and Palazzo del Governo. Rooms are equipped with air conditioning, a refrigerator, and free Wi-Fi. The hotel features a 24-hour front desk, outdoor furniture, and a sun terrace. Guests can also enjoy the on-site lounge and free public parking.
- Price: Approximately $25 per night.

4. Nissia Kamares (Kardamena)

Nissia Kamares offers tastefully furnished studios and apartments with spacious balconies overlooking green yards. Located in Kardamena, this guesthouse provides a pleasant and cozy atmosphere. Each unit includes a kitchenette, air conditioning, and free Wi-Fi. The property features a garden, a terrace, and a bar. Its quiet location and comfortable accommodations make it a popular choice for budget-conscious travelers.

- Price: Approximately $30 per night.

5. Fantasia Hotel Apartments (Kos Town)

Fantasia Hotel Apartments offers spacious and affordable accommodations in Kos Town. Each apartment includes a kitchenette, making it ideal for longer stays or those who prefer to prepare their own meals. The rooms are equipped with air conditioning, a TV, and free Wi-Fi. The hotel is close to the beach and local amenities, providing convenience and comfort for guests.

- Price: Approximately $40 per night.

These hostels and guesthouses provide comfortable and budget-friendly accommodations, making them perfect for travelers looking to explore Kos without breaking the bank.

Chapter 4. Top Attractions in Kos

- Asklepion of Kos

The Asklepion of Kos is one of the most famous and beautiful attractions on the island. It's an ancient healing temple dedicated to Asclepius, the Greek god of medicine. When you visit the Asklepion, you will be stepping back in time to the place where doctors once treated patients over 2,000 years ago.

As you arrive, you'll notice the ruins spread across different levels on a hillside. The view is stunning, with the sea and nearby mountains in the distance. It's a peaceful and scenic location, perfect for exploring at your own pace.

At the first level, you will find remains of rooms where people came to rest and heal. The ancient doctors believed in treating both the body and the mind, so the setting itself is calm and relaxing. You'll also see the remains of baths, where people came for cleansing and therapy.

As you walk up to the second level, you'll see the impressive ruins of the main temple dedicated to Asclepius. This was where sick people prayed for healing. The atmosphere here is truly special, and you can still feel the spiritual importance of the place.

Climbing to the top level, you'll be rewarded with breathtaking views of the Aegean Sea and Kos Town. It's a fantastic spot to take photos and soak in the island's beauty. You can sit for a moment and imagine how this place was once filled with people seeking help and relief.

The Asklepion is not only an important historical site but also a beautiful place to visit, offering a mix of culture, nature, and history. The combination of the ruins, the views, and the peaceful surroundings make it a truly enjoyable experience.

- Ancient Agora

The Ancient Agora of Kos is a must-visit if you enjoy history and exploring ancient ruins. Located right in Kos Town, this archaeological site was once the heart of the island's ancient city, bustling with people trading, gathering, and worshiping.

As you enter the site, you'll be amazed by the sheer size of the Agora. It's like stepping into an open-air museum, with ruins spread across a large area. You'll see the remains of ancient columns, walls, and pathways that once formed part of temples, shops, and public buildings. One of the highlights is the ruins of a temple dedicated to Hercules, one of the most famous heroes in Greek mythology. There's also a sanctuary dedicated to Aphrodite, the goddess of love and beauty.

Walking through the Agora, it's easy to imagine how lively this place must have been centuries ago, with markets, shops, and people going about their daily lives. You can explore the old stone roads that connect different parts of the site and wander through what was once a thriving marketplace.

As you move further into the site, you'll come across mosaics, remains of fountains, and ancient sculptures. These small details give you a glimpse of the artistry and culture of the people who lived here long ago. The combination of history and the peaceful atmosphere makes it a special place to wander around.

With its central location and easy access, the Ancient Agora is not only a fascinating place to visit but also a beautiful one. Surrounded by greenery and ancient stone, it's a quiet and scenic spot in the middle of the modern town, offering a perfect blend of past and present. It's a great place to walk through, take photos, and imagine the rich history of Kos unfolding before your eyes.

- Tree of Hippocrates

The Hippocrates tree in Kos has become a symbol of medical education and knowledge. Hippocrates is said to have taught his students under the tree, as well as Paul, who taught Christianity in Kos. The tree is an oriental plane tree, with a crown diameter of approximately 12 metres (40 feet), making it the largest plane tree in Europe. If you want to improve your medical knowledge or simply visit a location that has been important since ancient times, this should be on your itinerary!

Hippocrates' tree has stood in the center of Kos town for 2400 years. The current tree is only about 500 years old, but it could be a descendant of the original planted by Hippocrates of Kos between 2500 and 3000 BC. This ancient and majestic oak has hollowed out over time, and its branches are supported by metal scaffolding to prevent it from collapsing on passersby below.

- Roman Odeon

The Roman Odeon in Kos is a fascinating historical site that offers a glimpse into the island's rich Roman heritage. Located in the heart of Kos Town, this ancient theater was constructed in the 2nd century AD and is one of the most significant public buildings from that era.

The Odeon was originally built as a venue for musical competitions and public gatherings. It could accommodate up to 750 spectators and featured 14 rows of marble seats, nine of which have been restored[3]. The structure includes a circular orchestra with a marble mosaic floor and an irregular pentagon-shaped stage, adding to its architectural uniqueness.

Visitors can explore the well-preserved seating area, the underground corridors, and the display area featuring a photo exhibition from the Aegean Institute of Archaeological Studies[4]. The site is easily accessible and often hosts cultural events during the summer months, making it a vibrant part of Kos's cultural life.

If you're planning a visit, it's a good idea to go early or later in the day to avoid the crowds and fully immerse yourself in the history and beauty of the Roman Odeon.

- Neratzia Castle

Neratzia Castle, also known as the Castle of the Knights, is a prominent historical landmark on Kos Island. This imposing medieval fortress is located at the entrance of Kos Harbor and was constructed by the Knights of St. John between the 14th and 16th centuries.

The castle's name, "Neratzia," is derived from the bitter orange trees (nerantzia) that once surrounded the area1. The fortress was strategically built to protect the island and control the sea passage between Kos and the Turkish coast, particularly during the Crusades.

Neratzia Castle features two fortified enclosures: the inner and outer walls. The inner enclosure, which dates back to the late 14th century, includes a circular tower bearing the coats of arms of the Grand Masters of the Knights Hospitaller1. The outer enclosure was completed in the early 16th century and includes massive round bastions at the corners.

Visitors can explore the castle's impressive architecture, including its thick walls, towers, and the bridge that connects the castle to the mainland. The site also offers stunning views of the harbor and the surrounding area.

Although the castle is currently closed for renovations, it remains a significant historical site and a must-visit for anyone interested in the rich history of Kos Island.

- Zia Village

Zia, the highest village on the island of Kos, is located on the green northern slope of the Dikeos Mountains at an altitude of 325 meters and is surrounded by olive groves, cypresses, eucalyptus, and pine trees. This small town, home to less than 100 residents, is renowned for its fantastic views, especially at sunset, and is approximately 15 kilometers from the capital, Kos. On clear days, you can see the neighboring islands of Kalymnos and Pserimos, as well as the coast of Turkey. The lush green landscape is sustained by numerous water sources, making Zia a popular destination for both day tourists and sunset seekers. The village's narrow streets are lined with whitewashed houses, local artisan shops, and traditional tavernas offering delicious Greek cuisine. While it has become a tourist hotspot, Zia's charm remains, particularly at sunset, which is considered one of the most beautiful on the island. Visitors can reach Zia by public bus, rented vehicles, or as part of an island tour. The village also serves as a starting point for hiking trails, including a popular route to the Agios Ioannis Monastery. Not to be missed is the Watermill of Zia, a lesser-known spot offering homemade lemonade and a peaceful retreat from the busier areas.

- Thermes Hot Springs

Thermes Hot Springs is one of the most unique and popular natural attractions on Kos Island, located about 12 kilometers southeast of Kos Town. Nestled between rocky cliffs along the coastline, these thermal springs flow directly into the Aegean Sea, creating a natural pool where hot and cold waters mix, offering a therapeutic and relaxing experience. The water is rich in minerals such as calcium, magnesium, and potassium, believed to have healing properties for skin, joint pain, and stress relief.

Accessible by a short walk from the main road, Thermes offers stunning views of the surrounding cliffs and sea, making it a serene spot for unwinding. The springs are especially enjoyable in the early morning or evening when the temperatures are cooler. Visitors should note that the area around the hot springs is quite rocky, so sturdy shoes are recommended. Whether you're seeking wellness benefits or simply a peaceful place to soak in nature, a visit to Thermes Hot Springs is a must for any trip to Kos.

Chapter 5. Kos Island Towns and Villages

- Kos Town

Kos Town, located in the northeast, is a charming blend of modernity and history. This cosmopolitan hub is easily accessible and showcases the island's rich heritage through its streets, buildings, markets, parks, and squares.

Despite being a popular destination for tourists, especially during the extended season, Kos Town maintains a serene and orderly atmosphere. This is largely due to the widespread use of bicycles by both locals and visitors, contributing to its calm pace.

In the heart of the town, visitors can explore numerous historical sites. The town's cobblestone streets and alleys are lined with Greek, Roman, Byzantine, and Ottoman ruins, alongside impressive Italian-era buildings. This mix of ancient and modern elements creates a captivating, multicultural environment. As night falls, the beachfront area comes alive with cafes, bars, and restaurants, offering a lively and vibrant nightlife.

A unique aspect of Kos Town is its urban planning, implemented by the Italians after the 1933 earthquake. They focused on creating green spaces and parks, earning the town the nickname "garden city."

Kos Town offers a variety of entertainment and sightseeing options, including its picturesque harbor, the medieval Neratzia Castle, and an extensive network of bike lanes perfect for both short rides and longer excursions.

- Kardamena

Kardamena, a lively town on the southern coast of Kos Island, is known for its vibrant atmosphere, beautiful beaches, and rich history. Once a small fishing village, Kardamena has transformed into a popular tourist destination while still maintaining its local charm. Located about 30 kilometers from Kos Town and 7 kilometers from the airport, it is easily accessible and offers a mix of relaxation and entertainment.

The town's main attraction is its long sandy beach, stretching along the crystal-clear waters of the Aegean Sea. Beach bars, restaurants, and water sports facilities line the shore, making it a perfect spot for sunbathing, swimming, or trying out activities like jet skiing and windsurfing. In the evenings, Kardamena comes alive with a bustling nightlife, with numerous bars and clubs offering fun for visitors looking to enjoy the island's festive spirit.

Kardamena also has a rich history, with ruins of ancient temples and a small archaeological museum where visitors can learn about the town's past. The nearby Antimachia Castle, located on a hilltop overlooking the town, provides a glimpse into the medieval history of Kos and offers stunning panoramic views.

Kardamena is a must-visit destination on Kos Island If you're looking for a relaxing beach day, a night of fun, or a cultural experience.

- Kefalos

Kefalos is a picturesque town located on the western side of Kos Island, known for its traditional charm, stunning beaches, and historical significance. Perched on a hill, this quaint town offers panoramic views of the surrounding area, including the sweeping coastline and the islet of Kastri, which sits just off the shore. Once the ancient capital of Kos, Kefalos is steeped in history and offers visitors a peaceful retreat from the more bustling parts of the island.

One of Kefalos' main attractions is Agios Stefanos Beach, famous for its crystal-clear waters and the ancient ruins of a basilica that rest right on the shore. The nearby Paradise Beach, known for its soft sand and water sports, is another favorite for both tourists and locals.

Kefalos is also home to several important historical sites, including the remains of the Basilica of Agios Stefanos and the medieval Castle of Kefalos, both offering a glimpse into the town's rich past. Strolling through its narrow streets, visitors can discover charming tavernas serving traditional Greek dishes and local specialties like honey and wine.

With its blend of natural beauty, history, and authentic Greek hospitality, Kefalos is a must-visit destination for those looking to experience the more serene and cultural side of Kos Island.

- Tigaki

Tigaki is a serene seaside village perfect for soaking up Greece's warm sun and the clear waters of the Aegean Sea. Situated 11 kilometers from Kos Town and 7 kilometers north of Asfendiou village, Tigaki boasts an exotic landscape with palm trees and expansive beaches covered in fine golden sand. The main road along the beach is lined with relaxed bars and casual restaurants, while the side streets feature boutique hotels, apart-hotels, guest houses, and resorts. Getting to Tigaki is easy by car, taxi, bus, or motorbike via the main district road of Kos or a quieter, flat road ideal for cycling, starting from Faros in the Lambi area.

Tigaki Beach stretches for about 10 kilometers, with some areas organized near resorts and cafes, and others left more natural, offering sunbathers the chance to relax under the shade of trees. The winds in Tigaki can be frequent, making it a popular spot for windsurfing and kitesurfing. Additionally, a wide range of water sports and activities are available on the organized beaches. The shallow waters in some parts of Tigaki make it an ideal destination for families and energetic youngsters.

- Mastichari

Mastichari is a charming coastal village on the north coast of Kos, known for its relaxed vibe and beautiful beaches. Located about 22 kilometers from Kos Town and just 7 kilometers from the island's international airport, it is easily accessible and a favorite among visitors.

Scenic Beauty and Beaches

Mastichari boasts a wide, sandy beach that is perfect for sunbathing and swimming. The beach is well-organized with sun loungers, umbrellas, and several beach cafes that offer drinks and snacks right on the sand. The area is also popular for windsurfing and kitesurfing due to the favorable wind conditions.

Local Atmosphere

Despite its popularity, Mastichari has retained a laid-back and unpretentious atmosphere. The village center features family-run guesthouses, traditional tavernas, and shops, providing a welcoming and authentic Greek experience. The beachfront area is particularly inviting, with cafes and bars where you can relax and enjoy the view.

Activities and Excursions

Mastichari is not just about the beach. The village is a small port with regular ferries to the nearby islands of Kalymnos and Pserimos, making it a great base for island-hopping. The local fishing fleet adds to the village's charm, and fresh seafood is a highlight in many of the local restaurants.

Family-Friendly Environment

The shallow waters and soft sand make Mastichari an ideal destination for families with young children. There are also facilities like a volleyball pitch and a children's play area, ensuring that there is something for everyone.

Accessibility

Getting to Mastichari is straightforward, whether by car, taxi, or bus. The village is well-connected by road, and the proximity to the airport makes it a convenient destination for travelers.

Mastichari offers a perfect blend of relaxation, adventure, and local culture, making it a must-visit spot on the island of Kos.

- Antimachia

Antimachia, located in the center of Kos Island, is a traditional village with a rich history and a unique cultural heritage. Famous for its well-preserved **Antimachia Castle**, which dates back to the 14th century, the village offers visitors a chance to explore medieval ruins while enjoying panoramic views of the surrounding landscape. The castle, perched on a hill, was once a key defensive structure used by the Knights of St. John, and today, its impressive walls and towers still stand as a testament to its past.

In the heart of Antimachia, you'll find the **Antimachia Windmill**, one of the last remaining working windmills on the island. This iconic structure, which has been restored to its original condition, provides a glimpse into the island's agricultural traditions and is a popular spot for visitors to learn about Kos's history of grain production.

Antimachia is also home to a variety of charming local tavernas, where visitors can taste traditional Kos dishes and fresh produce from the surrounding farmlands. The village has a laid-back atmosphere, with friendly locals and a strong sense of community. Every year, it hosts various cultural festivals, celebrating local customs, music, and food.

With its combination of historical landmarks and traditional village life, Antimachia is an ideal destination for those looking to experience the authentic side of Kos Island away from the tourist crowds.

- Pyli

Pyli, a traditional village on Kos Island, is a charming destination known for its rich history and picturesque setting. Located about 15 kilometers southwest of Kos

Town and 10 kilometers from the island's airport, Pyli offers a serene escape with easy accessibility.

Historical Significance

Pyli is steeped in history, with its name tracing back to ancient times. The village is named after Palaio Pyli, an old settlement now in ruins. One of the notable historical sites is the **Paleo Pyli Castle**, a Byzantine fortress offering spectacular views of the surrounding landscape.

Village Life

The heart of Pyli is its central square, surrounded by traditional stone buildings, cafes, and tavernas. This area is the hub of local life, where you can enjoy a leisurely meal or a cup of coffee while soaking in the village's tranquil atmosphere[3]. The village also features charming shops, including art stores with locally made pottery, paintings, and jewelry.

Natural Beauty

Pyli is set against the backdrop of the Dikaios Mountains, providing a stunning natural setting. The village overlooks fertile lands, adding to its scenic beauty. Nearby, you can find the **Pyli Spring**, known for its lion-shaped water spouts, which is a popular spot for both locals and visitors.

Activities and Attractions
- - Paleo Pyli Castle: Explore the ruins of this ancient fortress and enjoy panoramic views.
- - Local Churches: Visit several Orthodox churches, including the Church of the Holy Cross and the oldest church in Pyli, Eisodia of the Theotokos.
- - Marmari Beach: Just a short drive away, this beach offers a perfect spot for relaxation and water activities.

Accessibility

Getting to Pyli is also straightforward, whether by car, taxi, or bus. The village's central location makes it a convenient base for exploring other parts of Kos Island.

Pyli is a blend of historical charm, natural beauty, and traditional Greek culture, making it a must-visit destination on Kos Island.

Chapter 6. Outdoor Activities and Nature

- Hiking and Nature Trails

Kos Island is not only known for its pristine beaches and rich historical sites but also for its stunning natural landscapes and diverse terrain, which makes it a perfect destination for hiking enthusiasts. From coastal walks with panoramic sea views to mountainous paths through lush forests, Kos offers a variety of hiking and nature trails that cater to all levels of experience. Hiking on Kos provides an opportunity to explore the island's unspoiled beauty, discover hidden gems, and experience local culture in its purest form.

1. Dikeos Mountain Trail

One of the most popular and rewarding hikes on the island is the trail that leads to Mount Dikeos, the highest peak on Kos at 846 meters. This hike begins in the picturesque village of Zia, located on the northern slopes of the mountain. Zia is well-known for its stunning sunsets and traditional charm, making it a perfect starting point for this adventure.

The trail offers a mix of rugged terrain, forested areas, and open views of the island and the surrounding Aegean Sea. As you ascend, you'll pass through pine forests, olive groves, and fields filled with wildflowers, especially vibrant during spring. Reaching the summit of Mount Dikeos rewards hikers with breathtaking panoramic views of Kos, the neighboring islands of Kalymnos and Pserimos, and even the coast of Turkey on a clear day. The hike takes about 3-4 hours round trip, depending on your pace, and is best attempted in the early morning or late afternoon to avoid the midday heat.

2. Old Pyli to Pyli Castle

Another excellent hiking route is the trail from Old Pyli to Pyli Castle. Old Pyli is a ghost village that offers a glimpse into Kos's past, with its abandoned houses and narrow, stone-paved streets. The hike begins in this deserted village, situated on a hillside, and takes you through olive groves and terraced fields to the medieval ruins of Pyli Castle.

The trail is moderately challenging but suitable for most hikers. As you climb towards the castle, you'll be treated to stunning views of the surrounding valleys and the Aegean coastline. Pyli Castle, once a fortified stronghold, now offers an excellent vantage point for photography and exploration. The hike also provides opportunities to see local wildlife, including birds and small mammals. This trail takes about 2-3 hours round trip and can be extended by exploring nearby natural springs and the Tomb of Harmylos.

3. Asfendiou to Zia

For those looking for a leisurely yet scenic hike, the route from Asfendiou to Zia is ideal. Asfendiou is a small village situated on the lower slopes of Mount Dikeos, known for its traditional Greek architecture and peaceful surroundings. The hike from Asfendiou to Zia is a gentle uphill walk along a well-marked path that meanders through olive groves and vineyards.

This trail offers a more relaxed hiking experience while still providing stunning views of the island's northern coast and distant islands. Along the way, you'll pass small chapels and ruins of ancient farmhouses, offering insight into the agricultural history of the island. Once you reach Zia, you can explore the village's artisan shops and traditional tavernas, or relax and enjoy the famous sunset. The hike takes about 1-2 hours one way, making it perfect for a half-day excursion.

4. Plaka Forest and Paradise Beach

For nature lovers, a hike through Plaka Forest combined with a visit to Paradise Beach offers a unique experience of Kos's diverse ecosystem. Plaka Forest, located near the town of Antimachia, is a peaceful pine forest that serves as a natural habitat for peacocks and other wildlife. The forest is crisscrossed with several easy walking trails, making it perfect for a leisurely hike or a family outing.

After exploring the forest, you can continue your hike down towards Paradise Beach, one of the island's most famous beaches, known for its clear waters and fine sand. The contrast between the dense, shaded forest and the sunny coastline makes this hike particularly enjoyable. The total hike, including time spent relaxing at the beach, takes about 3-4 hours.

5. Therma Hot Springs to Agios Fokas
For those interested in coastal hiking, the trail from Therma Hot Springs to Agios Fokas offers a combination of seaside views and geological wonders. The hike begins at the famous hot springs, where thermal waters meet the Aegean Sea, creating natural pools for soaking and relaxation. From there, the path follows the coastline, with stunning views of the rocky cliffs and the open sea.

The trail leads to the small beach of Agios Fokas, a quiet spot perfect for swimming or picnicking. Along the way, hikers can explore volcanic rock formations, hidden coves, and patches of wild herbs that grow along the shore. This easy coastal hike is about 2-3 hours round trip and is ideal for those looking for a scenic yet relaxing walk.

6. Lagoudi Village to Amaniou Monastery

For a more spiritual and serene hiking experience, the trail from Lagoudi Village to the Amaniou Monastery is a peaceful journey through the island's religious heritage and natural beauty. Lagoudi is a small, traditional village known for its quiet streets and beautiful views. The hike from Lagoudi to the monastery is a moderate uphill climb that takes you through forests and open meadows, offering a chance to see local flora and fauna along the way.

The Amaniou Monastery, located in a secluded spot on the hillside, is an old and tranquil place of worship, offering breathtaking views of the island and surrounding sea. The hike takes about 2-3 hours round trip and provides an opportunity to reflect and relax in a peaceful setting far from the hustle and bustle of the island's tourist spots.

Practical Tips for Hiking in Kos

- - Best Time to Hike: The best seasons for hiking in Kos are spring and autumn, as the weather is mild and the landscapes are lush with blooming flowers. Summer can be very hot, so if hiking during this time, it's recommended to start early in the morning or late in the afternoon.
- - What to Bring: Make sure to wear sturdy shoes, bring plenty of water, sunscreen, a hat, and snacks for longer hikes. In some areas, the terrain can be rocky, so proper footwear is essential.
- - Local Guidance: If you're unfamiliar with the trails, consider joining a guided hiking tour, as local guides can provide insights into the island's history, wildlife, and natural features.
- - Respect Nature: Always stay on marked trails, respect wildlife, and take any trash with you to preserve the island's natural beauty.

Kos Island offers a variety of hiking and nature trails that showcase its diverse landscapes and rich cultural heritage.

- Water Sports and Diving

Kos Island, with its crystal-clear waters and expansive coastlines, is a haven for water sports enthusiasts and divers alike. Whether you're seeking high-adrenaline activities like windsurfing or kiteboarding, or you want to explore the serene underwater world through diving or snorkeling, Kos offers an abundance of options for water-based adventures. Its ideal weather conditions, modern facilities, and pristine marine environment make it a perfect destination for all kinds of water sports.

1. Windsurfing and Kitesurfing
Kos is renowned for its strong winds, especially in the northern part of the island, which make it an excellent spot for windsurfing and kitesurfing. The consistent winds, especially during the summer months, create the

ideal conditions for both beginners and experienced surfers.

- Mastichari Beach is one of the best spots for windsurfing on the island, with reliable winds and shallow waters. There are several windsurfing schools and rental shops along the beach, offering lessons and equipment for all levels.
- Kardamena Beach is another hotspot for both windsurfing and kitesurfing, with long stretches of sandy beach and strong winds throughout the day. The beach caters to various skill levels, with schools providing professional guidance and equipment rentals.
- Psalidi Beach, located close to Kos Town, is also popular for windsurfing due to its frequent winds and calm waters, making it a great spot for beginners. Kitesurfing enthusiasts will find the northern part of Psalidi beach to be ideal for practicing jumps and tricks.

2. Snorkeling

For those who prefer a more relaxed water activity, snorkeling is a fantastic way to explore the marine life around Kos. The island's clear waters provide excellent visibility, making it easy to discover the rich underwater world filled with colorful fish, sea urchins, and other marine creatures.

- Agios Stefanos Beach is a top spot for snorkeling, especially around the ancient ruins of the Basilica of Agios Stefanos, where underwater rock formations shelter a variety of sea life.
- Limnionas Bay, located on the western coast, offers calm and clear waters that are perfect for snorkeling. The bay is relatively quiet, making it ideal for those who want to explore the underwater world at a more relaxed pace.
- Camel Beach is another hidden gem, offering beautiful rock formations beneath the water, where you can encounter various fish and sea creatures.

3. Scuba Diving

Kos is an excellent destination for scuba diving, with dive sites that cater to both beginners and advanced divers. The island's surrounding waters are home to a variety of marine life, including octopuses, barracudas, and moray eels. There are also numerous caves, shipwrecks, and ancient underwater ruins to explore.

- The Bubble Beach in Kefalos is a unique diving spot, known for its underwater bubbles that rise from volcanic activity beneath the surface. Divers can swim through these bubbles and explore the surrounding underwater environment, which is teeming with life.
- The Nisyros Island Dive is one of the most exciting scuba diving experiences in the area. This dive takes place around the volcanic island of Nisyros, which is a short boat trip from Kos. The underwater volcanic formations are impressive, and divers often encounter a wide array of marine species.
- The Kastri Islet Dive, just off the coast of Kefalos, is another excellent spot for exploring marine life and underwater caves. The small islet offers several dive sites that range from shallow areas perfect for beginners to deeper sites with caves and rock formations for more advanced divers.

There are several reputable dive centers across the island, particularly in Kos Town, Kefalos, and Mastichari, offering guided dives, certification courses, and equipment rental for all levels of experience. Many diving schools also provide training for beginners, allowing first-timers to safely experience the wonders of the underwater world.

4. Jet Skiing and Water Skiing
For thrill-seekers, jet skiing and water skiing are popular activities available at many of Kos's beaches. The island's calm waters and extensive coastline offer perfect conditions for these high-speed water sports.

- Tigaki Beach and Kardamena Beach are among the best spots for jet skiing, with rental services and designated areas for safe riding. Jet skiing provides an exhilarating way to explore the coastline, with opportunities to ride through calm waters or challenge the waves further out to sea.
- Water skiing is also available at several beaches, with lessons and equipment rentals provided for both

beginners and experienced skiers. The smooth waters of Psalidi Beach make it an ideal spot for this sport.

5. Stand-Up Paddleboarding (SUP)

Stand-up paddleboarding (SUP) has gained popularity in recent years and is a great way to explore the island's coastline at a relaxed pace. This activity is suitable for all ages and fitness levels, as it allows participants to enjoy the sea while standing on a large board and using a paddle to glide through the water.

- Mastichari Beach and Kamari Bay offer calm and clear waters, making them perfect locations for stand-up paddleboarding. Whether you're paddling near the shore or venturing out to explore hidden coves, SUP provides a peaceful and scenic way to enjoy the natural beauty of Kos.
- For those seeking a more adventurous experience, Limnionas Beach offers slightly rougher waters and rockier coastlines, providing a thrilling challenge for more experienced paddleboarders.

6. Kayaking and Canoeing

Kayaking and canoeing are excellent ways to discover the hidden coves, sea caves, and remote beaches of Kos. These activities allow you to access areas that are difficult to reach by foot or car, providing an intimate experience with the island's natural beauty.

- Kefalos Bay is a popular spot for kayaking, offering calm waters and stunning views of the surrounding landscape. Paddling along the coast, you can explore the small islets, including Kastri Island, which is home to a charming chapel.
- Therma Beach is another excellent location for kayaking, particularly for those looking to combine adventure with relaxation. After exploring the coastline by kayak, you can enjoy a soak in the nearby hot springs.

Guided kayaking tours are available for those who want to explore more remote areas of the island, including the rugged coastline near Limnionas and the quiet beaches on the northern side of the island.

Practical Tips for Water Sports and Diving

- Safety First: Always use the necessary safety equipment, including life vests and helmets for sports like jet skiing and water skiing. Make sure to follow the instructions of your instructors or guides to ensure a safe and enjoyable experience.

- Best Time for Water Sports: The best time for water sports in Kos is during the summer months (June to September), when the weather is warm, and the sea conditions are perfect. However, diving is available year-round, with some sites offering the best visibility during the shoulder seasons (April to May, and September to October).

- Choose Licensed Providers: Whether you're renting equipment or taking lessons, ensure that you're using licensed and reputable service providers. This guarantees not only safety but also high-quality equipment and professional guidance.

Kos Island offers an unparalleled range of water sports and diving opportunities for visitors seeking adventure, relaxation, or exploration. With its warm waters, diverse marine life, and excellent facilities, the island is a water sports paradise, catering to everyone from beginners to experienced athletes.

- Cycling Routes

Kos Island is a fantastic destination for cycling enthusiasts, boasting a wide variety of cycling routes that showcase its stunning landscapes, charming villages, historical sites, and beautiful coastlines. With a generally flat terrain along the coast and hilly areas inland, Kos offers routes suitable for both beginners and more experienced cyclists. The island's well-maintained paths, combined with excellent weather conditions, make cycling one of the most enjoyable ways to explore its natural beauty and cultural heritage.

1. Kos Town to Tigaki Beach

One of the most popular and easy routes on the island, the Kos Town to Tigaki Beach ride is perfect for families and casual cyclists. This 10 km (6 miles) route runs along the coast and offers picturesque views of the Aegean Sea.

- Starting Point: Kos Town
- Distance: 10 km (6 miles) one way
- Difficulty: Easy
- Route Highlights: The ride takes you through flat terrain with views of the sea, passing through small villages and olive groves before reaching the sandy Tigaki Beach. Once there, cyclists can relax by the beach or enjoy a meal at one of the seaside tavernas.
- Tip: The path is well-paved, making it ideal for beginners or families with children. Tigaki Beach is known for its shallow waters, so it's a great spot to take a break and swim.

2. Kos Town to Psalidi

This easy, short route is ideal for those wanting to explore the outskirts of Kos Town while staying close to the sea. The coastal path offers a relaxed ride with beautiful views of the water.

- Starting Point: Kos Town
- Distance: 6 km (3.7 miles) one way
- Difficulty: Easy
- Route Highlights: The route passes through Kos Marina and follows a flat coastal path all the way to Psalidi Beach. Cyclists can stop for a swim at any of the small beaches along the way or continue to Psalidi for a meal at one of the seaside restaurants.
- Tip: This route is ideal for casual riders looking to enjoy a leisurely day of cycling and sightseeing.

3. Zia to Pyli

For those seeking a more challenging ride, the mountainous inland areas of Kos provide an exhilarating adventure. The route from Zia to Pyli is a rewarding challenge that takes cyclists through scenic landscapes with panoramic views of the island.

- Starting Point: Zia Village
- Distance: 12 km (7.5 miles)
- Difficulty: Moderate to difficult

- Route Highlights: Zia, the highest village on Kos, offers fantastic views and is a great place to start a more demanding ride. The route descends toward Pyli, passing olive groves, forests, and scenic viewpoints. Pyli, a traditional village, is known for its quaint streets and historical landmarks, such as the Pyli Fountain.
- Tip: This route includes some uphill sections, so it's better suited for experienced cyclists. It's also an excellent opportunity to explore Kos's traditional mountain villages.

4. Kardamena to Antimachia

A relatively easy yet scenic route, the ride from Kardamena to Antimachia takes cyclists through rolling hills and rural areas, offering a glimpse of the island's agricultural heart.

- Starting Point: Kardamena
- Distance: 7 km (4.3 miles)
- Difficulty: Easy to moderate
- Route Highlights: Starting from the coastal town of Kardamena, the route gently climbs toward Antimachia,

a village known for its traditional windmill and the Antimachia Castle. Along the way, cyclists can enjoy views of the countryside, passing vineyards, olive groves, and farmlands.

- Tip: The route is well-suited for cyclists of all levels and provides a nice balance between coastal and rural scenery. Don't miss a stop at the windmill in Antimachia for a taste of local history.

5. Kos Town to Mastichari

For cyclists who want a longer coastal ride, the route from Kos Town to Mastichari is an excellent choice. This 24 km (15 miles) route runs along the northern coast of the island, offering beautiful sea views, traditional villages, and beach stops.

- Starting Point: Kos Town
- Distance: 24 km (15 miles) one way
- Difficulty: Moderate
- Route Highlights: This route follows a relatively flat terrain and passes through villages like Tigaki and Marmari, providing plenty of opportunities for rest stops.

Mastichari is a charming seaside town with sandy beaches and is known for its seafood tavernas, making it a perfect spot to relax after the ride.

- Tip: This route is great for those looking to cover more distance while staying on mostly flat terrain. It's perfect for a day-long cycling trip, with time for beach breaks and lunch at Mastichari.

6. Kefalos Loop

For experienced cyclists, the Kefalos Loop is a challenging yet highly rewarding route. It takes you through the hilly and rugged landscape of the Kefalos Peninsula, offering stunning views of the sea and remote, peaceful beaches.

- Starting Point: Kefalos Village
- Distance: 40 km (25 miles) loop
- Difficulty: Difficult
- Route Highlights: This loop takes you around the Kefalos Peninsula, passing through scenic countryside, traditional villages, and hidden beaches like Agios Stefanos. The ride offers breathtaking views of the

surrounding islands and the Aegean Sea. For those looking for a challenging climb, the route also includes sections with significant elevation changes.
- Tip: The Kefalos Loop is ideal for advanced cyclists looking for a challenge. Make sure to bring plenty of water, as some stretches of the route are quite remote.

7. Therma Beach Route
A ride to the unique Therma Hot Springs is a rewarding experience for cyclists looking to combine nature, adventure, and relaxation.

- Starting Point: Kos Town
- Distance: 10 km (6 miles) one way
- Difficulty: Moderate
- Route Highlights: The route follows a coastal path with some uphill sections, leading to the famous Therma Beach, known for its natural hot springs. The beach is located in a secluded area, offering a quiet and relaxing environment for a dip in the therapeutic waters.

- Tip: This route is suitable for intermediate cyclists. Make sure to pack swimwear so you can enjoy the hot springs at the end of your ride.

Practical Tips for Cycling in Kos
- Best Time to Cycle: The best time for cycling in Kos is from spring (April) to early autumn (October), when the weather is pleasant, and the island is in full bloom. Summer can be very hot, so early morning or late afternoon rides are recommended during this season.
- Safety First: Always wear a helmet and bring plenty of water, especially if cycling during the warmer months. Sunscreen and sunglasses are also essential for protection from the sun.
- Bike Rentals: Kos has many bike rental shops, particularly in Kos Town and popular tourist areas like Kardamena and Tigaki. You can choose from a variety of bikes, including road bikes, mountain bikes, and electric bikes.
- Respect Nature: Some routes take you through natural reserves and rural areas. Be respectful of the

environment by staying on designated paths and taking all your trash with you.

- Guided Tours: If you're new to the island or want to explore more remote areas, there are several companies offering guided cycling tours that provide insight into the island's history, culture, and natural beauty.

Kos Island is a cyclist's paradise, with its diverse terrain, scenic routes, and perfect climate for outdoor activities. Whether you're a beginner or an experienced cyclist, the island offers a range of cycling routes that allow you to explore its stunning landscapes, historical sites, and coastal beauty.

- Guided Tours and Excursions

Kos Island offers a wide array of guided tours and excursions that give visitors the opportunity to explore its rich history, beautiful landscapes, and vibrant culture. From ancient archaeological sites to secluded beaches and hidden gems, guided tours offer an insightful and convenient way to experience the best of the island.

1. Historical and Cultural Tours

Kos Island is steeped in history, and a guided tour of its most famous historical sites is a must for culture enthusiasts. Professional guides provide fascinating insights into the island's rich past, connecting you to the ancient civilizations that once thrived here.

- Highlights:

 - Asklepion of Kos: Visit the ancient healing temple, one of the most significant archaeological sites on the island. Learn about Hippocrates, the father of medicine, who is said to have practiced here.

 - Kos Town Walking Tour: Stroll through the heart of Kos Town, exploring its historical monuments such as the Neratzia Castle, the Ancient Agora, and the Roman Odeon. The tour typically includes visits to medieval landmarks and Byzantine churches.

 - Zia Village Cultural Tour: Discover the traditional village of Zia on a cultural tour. You'll walk through narrow streets lined with artisan shops and get the chance to experience local life, traditions, and crafts.

2. Boat Excursions

Kos is surrounded by stunning waters and picturesque neighboring islands, making boat excursions one of the best ways to explore the Aegean Sea. These guided boat tours offer everything from day trips to nearby islands to snorkeling adventures and sunset cruises.

- Highlights:

- Day Trip to Kalymnos, Pserimos, and Plati: Set sail on a traditional Greek boat to explore the nearby islands. Kalymnos is known for its sponge diving history, while Pserimos offers secluded beaches and crystal-clear waters. Enjoy swimming, snorkeling, and relaxing on the deck as you cruise between islands.

- Nisyros Volcano Tour: Take a boat trip to the volcanic island of Nisyros and explore its still-active crater. Walk across the lunar-like landscape of the Stefanos Crater and visit the charming village of Mandraki.

- Sunset Cruise: Embark on a romantic sunset cruise along the coast of Kos. Watch the sky light up with hues of orange and pink as the sun sets behind the Dikeos

Mountains. Some tours include a dinner or wine-tasting experience on board.

3. Hiking and Nature Tours
Kos is a hiker's paradise, with guided hiking tours offering an immersive experience in the island's natural beauty. From easy walks to more challenging hikes, these excursions take you to some of the most scenic spots on the island.

- Highlights:

- Mount Dikeos Hiking Tour: Join a guided hike to the summit of Mount Dikeos, the highest point on the island, for panoramic views of Kos and the surrounding islands. Along the way, you'll pass through pine forests and charming villages like Zia.

- Kos Countryside Walking Tour: Explore the lush countryside on foot, discovering hidden springs, olive groves, and traditional farmhouses. These tours often include stops at local farms, where you can sample fresh produce and learn about traditional farming methods.

4. Food and Wine Tours

Food lovers will enjoy guided culinary tours that introduce you to the island's rich flavors. Kos is known for its fresh produce, traditional recipes, and locally-produced wines, and these tours offer a taste of authentic Greek cuisine.

- Highlights:

- Wine Tasting in Mastichari: Visit local vineyards in the Mastichari region, where you can sample wines made from indigenous grape varieties. Learn about the winemaking process and enjoy tastings of reds, whites, and rosés paired with local cheeses and olives.

- Traditional Cooking Class in Zia: Take a hands-on cooking class in the village of Zia. Learn how to prepare classic Kos dishes like moussaka, saganaki, and tzatziki from local chefs. After the class, enjoy the fruits of your labor with a glass of local wine.

- Olive Oil and Honey Tasting: Discover the flavors of Kos on a food tour that includes visits to olive oil mills and honey farms. Taste the island's famous thyme honey and sample extra virgin olive oil made from ancient olive groves.

5. Adventure and Water Sports Tours

For those seeking adventure, Kos offers an abundance of guided tours focused on outdoor activities and water sports. Whether you're a seasoned adventurer or just looking to try something new, these tours provide excitement and fun in the sun.

- Highlights:

 - Scuba Diving Excursions: Dive into the crystal-clear waters of the Aegean with a guided scuba diving tour. Explore underwater caves, reefs, and ancient shipwrecks, with opportunities for both beginner and advanced divers.

 - Windsurfing and Kitesurfing: Kos is known for its excellent windsurfing and kitesurfing conditions. Join a guided tour for lessons or hire equipment and head to popular spots like Psalidi Beach or Mastichari.

 - Jeep Safari Adventure: Discover the rugged terrain of Kos on a guided Jeep safari. You'll travel off-road through mountain paths, dense forests, and remote villages, with plenty of stops for photos and swimming along the way.

6. Religious and Pilgrimage Tours
Kos has a rich religious heritage, and guided pilgrimage tours offer a deep dive into the island's spiritual history. These tours often include visits to important religious landmarks, monasteries, and chapels.

- Highlights:

- Agios Ioannis Monastery Tour: Visit the Monastery of Agios Ioannis, located in a remote area near Zia. This peaceful retreat offers stunning views and an opportunity to learn about the island's Christian heritage.

- Church of Agia Paraskevi: Explore the island's largest church, located in Kos Town. The Church of Agia Paraskevi is an important religious site, known for its beautiful frescoes and icons.

Chapter 7. Food and Drink on Kos Island

- Traditional Kos Cuisine

1. Krasotyri (Wine Cheese)

Krasotyri, also known as "Posa cheese," is a distinctive cheese made from sheep or goat's milk. Its unique maturation process involves soaking the cheese in red wine, which imparts a rich, tangy flavor and a striking dark red exterior. This traditional cheese is a staple in Kos and is often enjoyed with fresh bread, olives, and tomatoes as part of a meze platter. The wine infusion not only enhances the taste but also preserves the cheese, making it a delightful and long-lasting treat. Krasotyri is a must-try for cheese lovers visiting the island.

2. Pitaridia

Pitaridia is a beloved traditional pasta dish from Kos, made from hand-rolled dough similar to lasagna sheets. The pasta is boiled in a flavorful meat broth, which infuses it with a rich, savory taste. Once cooked, it's typically served with a generous topping of melted butter and grated cheese, creating a comforting and hearty meal. Pitaridia is often prepared for special occasions and family gatherings, reflecting the island's culinary traditions. The dish's simplicity and depth of flavor make it a favorite among locals and visitors alike, offering a taste of authentic Greek home cooking.

3. Katimeria

Katimeria are delightful small pies made with thin layers of dough and filled with local cheese, such as myzithra. These pies are typically fried until golden and crispy, then drizzled with honey and sprinkled with cinnamon, creating a perfect balance of sweet and savory flavors. Katimeria are often enjoyed as a dessert or a sweet snack, especially during festive occasions and celebrations. Their delicate texture and rich filling make them a popular treat among both locals and tourists. Each bite of katimeria offers a taste of Kos's culinary heritage and the island's love for sweet delicacies.

4. Chtapodokeftedes (Octopus Balls)

Chtapodokeftedes, or octopus balls, are a savory delicacy from Kos. The octopus is finely chopped and mixed with a blend of herbs, spices, and sometimes breadcrumbs, then formed into small balls and fried until crispy on the outside and tender on the inside. These flavorful bites are typically served as an appetizer or part of a meze platter, accompanied by a squeeze of lemon and a side of tzatziki or other dipping sauces. Chtapodokeftedes are a testament to the island's rich seafood tradition and are a must-try for anyone looking to experience authentic Greek flavors.

5. Stuffed Zucchini Flowers

Stuffed zucchini flowers are a popular and delicate dish in Kos. The flowers are carefully filled with a mixture of rice, fresh herbs like dill and mint, and sometimes cheese, then lightly fried or baked to perfection. This dish showcases the island's use of fresh, local ingredients and its culinary creativity. The result is a flavorful and aromatic treat that is both light and satisfying. Stuffed zucchini flowers are often served as an appetizer or a side dish, offering a taste of the island's garden-fresh produce and traditional cooking techniques.

6. Pasha Macaroni

Pasha Macaroni is a traditional dish from Kos that features thick pasta cooked in a rich meat broth. The pasta absorbs the flavors of the broth, resulting in a hearty and savory meal. Often, pieces of tender meat are added to the dish, enhancing its richness. The final touch is a generous topping of grated cheese, which melts into the pasta, creating a creamy and satisfying texture. Pasha Macaroni is typically enjoyed during festive occasions and family gatherings, reflecting the island's culinary traditions and the importance of communal meals in Greek culture.

7. Lambropites

Lambropites are small, savory pies made with myzithra cheese, a soft and creamy cheese from Kos. These pies are traditionally prepared during Easter and other festive occasions. The dough is rolled out thin and filled with the cheese mixture, then folded and baked until golden brown. Lambropites can be either sweet or savory, depending on the addition of ingredients like honey or herbs. They are often enjoyed as a snack or appetizer, showcasing the island's love for cheese and baked goods. Each bite of lambropites offers a taste of Kos's rich culinary heritage.

8. Dolmades

Dolmades are a staple in Greek cuisine, and the version from Kos is particularly delicious. These vine leaves are stuffed with a mixture of rice, fresh herbs such as dill and mint, and sometimes minced meat. The stuffed leaves are then simmered in a flavorful broth until tender. Dolmades are typically served as an appetizer or part of a meze platter, often accompanied by a squeeze of lemon and a dollop of yogurt. The combination of the tender vine leaves and the aromatic filling makes dolmades a beloved dish that reflects the island's culinary traditions.

9. Pork Cooked with Coarse Oatmeal

This hearty dish features pork cooked slowly with coarse oatmeal, resulting in a rich and flavorful meal. The pork is typically marinated with herbs and spices before being simmered with the oatmeal, which absorbs the meat's juices and flavors. The dish is often served with a side of vegetables or bread, making it a satisfying and nourishing meal. This traditional recipe showcases the island's agricultural heritage and the use of locally sourced ingredients. Pork cooked with coarse oatmeal is a comforting dish that reflects the rustic and hearty nature of Kos's cuisine.

10. Thyme Honey

Thyme honey from Kos is renowned for its aromatic flavor and is a must-try for visitors to the island. The honey is produced by bees that feed on the abundant thyme plants found in the region, resulting in a product with a distinct and fragrant taste. Thyme honey is often used in desserts, drizzled over yogurt, or enjoyed with bread. Its unique flavor makes it a versatile ingredient in both sweet and savory dishes. The production of thyme honey is a testament to the island's rich natural resources and the importance of beekeeping in Kos's agricultural traditions.

- Best Local Restaurants

1. Taverna Romeo

Taverna Romeo is a beloved local spot known for its warm hospitality and delicious Greek cuisine. Located in Psalidi, this family-run taverna offers a cozy atmosphere with outdoor seating that overlooks the sea. The menu features a variety of traditional dishes, including fresh seafood, grilled meats, and vegetarian options. Signature dishes like moussaka, souvlaki, and Greek salad are prepared with fresh, locally sourced ingredients. The friendly staff and live Greek music add to the authentic dining experience, making Taverna Romeo a must-visit for anyone looking to enjoy a true taste of Kos.

2. Patriko

Patriko, located in Kos Town, is a charming family restaurant that offers high-quality traditional Greek cuisine. The cozy atmosphere and outstanding service make it a favorite among locals and tourists alike. The menu includes a wide range of meze, grilled meats, and seafood dishes, all prepared with fresh, local ingredients. Patriko is particularly known for its lamb kleftiko and stuffed vine leaves. The reasonable prices and generous portions ensure a satisfying dining experience. Whether you're looking for a casual meal or a special dinner, Patriko provides a welcoming and delicious option.

3. Ampeli

Ampeli, situated in Tigaki, offers a unique dining experience with its focus on Greek and Eastern Mediterranean cuisine. Located in a picturesque vineyard, the restaurant provides a serene and beautiful setting for a meal. The menu features a variety of dishes made with fresh, seasonal ingredients, including grilled meats, seafood, and vegetarian options. Signature dishes like lamb chops, octopus, and various meze are complemented by a selection of local wines. The combination of excellent food, stunning views, and a relaxed atmosphere makes Ampeli a standout choice for dining in Kos.

4. Angelica's Beach Taverna

Angelica's Beach Taverna, located at Lambi Beach, is the perfect spot for a leisurely lunch by the sea. This charming taverna offers a variety of traditional Greek dishes, including fresh seafood, salads, and grilled meats. The beachfront location provides stunning views and a relaxed atmosphere, making it an ideal place to unwind and enjoy a meal. Popular dishes include grilled octopus, calamari, and Greek salad, all prepared with fresh, local ingredients. The friendly service and beautiful setting make Angelica's Beach Taverna a favorite among visitors to Kos.

5. Jenny Camel Restaurant

Jenny Camel Restaurant, located at Camel Beach, offers traditional Greek food with a stunning view of the sea. The restaurant is known for its fresh seafood, grilled meats, and homemade desserts. The menu features a variety of dishes made with locally sourced ingredients, including favorites like grilled fish, lamb chops, and baklava. The outdoor seating area provides a perfect spot to enjoy a meal while taking in the beautiful surroundings. The combination of delicious food, friendly service, and breathtaking views makes Jenny Camel Restaurant a must-visit on Kos.

- Local Markets and Street Food

1. Kos Town Market

The Kos Town Market, located in Eleftherias Square, is a bustling hub of local activity. This indoor market is housed in a historic building from the 1930s, featuring Italian architectural design. Here, you'll find a wide variety of fresh produce, including fruits, vegetables, herbs, and spices. The market is also known for its local products such as olive oil, honey, and traditional sweets. It's a great place to pick up souvenirs, with stalls selling handmade crafts, ceramics, and textiles. The vibrant atmosphere and the array of goods make Kos Town Market a must-visit for anyone exploring the island.

2. Zia Village Market

Zia Village, nestled in the Dikaios Mountains, is famous for its charming market. The market is a treasure trove of local crafts, including handmade jewelry, pottery, and textiles. Visitors can also find a variety of local delicacies, such as honey, olive oil, and herbs. The market is particularly lively in the evenings, with vendors setting up stalls along the narrow streets. The picturesque setting, combined with the unique products on offer, makes Zia Village Market a delightful place to shop and experience the local culture.

3. Antimachia Market

Antimachia Market is a smaller, yet equally charming market located in the village of Antimachia. This market is known for its fresh produce, including fruits, vegetables, and herbs grown in the fertile lands of Kos. You can also find local cheeses, olives, and traditional baked goods. The market is a great place to interact with local farmers and artisans, offering a glimpse into the island's agricultural heritage. The friendly atmosphere and high-quality products make Antimachia Market a favorite among locals and visitors alike.

4. Kardamena Market

Kardamena Market, situated in the lively town of Kardamena, offers a mix of fresh produce, local products, and souvenirs. The market is known for its vibrant atmosphere, with vendors selling everything from fruits and vegetables to handmade crafts and jewelry. Street food stalls are also a highlight, offering delicious local snacks such as souvlaki, gyros, and loukoumades (Greek doughnuts). The market is a great place to experience the local culture and enjoy some of the island's best street food.

5. Tigaki Market

Tigaki Market is a popular spot for both locals and tourists, located in the seaside village of Tigaki. The market features a variety of stalls selling fresh produce, local delicacies, and handmade crafts. Visitors can find everything from fresh fruits and vegetables to traditional sweets and pastries. The market is also known for its friendly vendors and relaxed atmosphere, making it a pleasant place to shop and explore. The proximity to the beach adds to the appeal, allowing visitors to combine a day of shopping with a relaxing beach outing.

- Wine and Olive Oil Tasting

Kos Island offers a delightful experience for wine and olive oil enthusiasts, with several local producers providing tours and tastings.

1. Hatziemmanouil Winery

Hatziemmanouil Winery, located near Asfendiou, has been producing wine for over a century. The family-owned vineyard covers 80 acres and benefits from the semi-tropical climate and Aegean breeze. Visitors can tour the modern winery, learn about the winemaking process, and enjoy tastings of their exceptional wines. The winery's courtyard, with views of the vineyards and the sea, provides a perfect setting for a relaxing wine tasting experience.

2. Ktima Akrani

Ktima Akrani, an award-winning organic winery, is situated at the foothills of Mount Dikaios. Established in 2001, the winery uses modern techniques to produce high-quality wines. Visitors can tour the vineyard and winery, learning about organic farming practices and the winemaking process. Tastings include a variety of wines, allowing guests to appreciate the unique flavors of Kos's terroir. The serene setting and knowledgeable guides make Ktima Akrani a must-visit for wine lovers.

3. Kos Olive Oil Tasting and Farm Tour

This tour offers an immersive experience into the world of olive oil production on Kos. Visitors can explore local olive groves, learn about traditional and modern olive oil extraction methods, and participate in tastings. The tour often includes a visit to a local farm, where guests can enjoy a meal featuring fresh, local ingredients and sample different varieties of olive oil. This experience provides a deeper understanding of the significance of olive oil in Kos's gastronomy and culture.

4. Kos Local Tasting – Wine, Oil & Honey

This comprehensive tasting experience allows visitors to explore the flavors of Kos through wine, olive oil, and honey. The tour includes visits to local vineyards and olive oil producers, where guests can learn about the production processes and sample a variety of products. The honey tasting session highlights the island's beekeeping traditions and the unique flavors of Kos's thyme honey. This tour offers a well-rounded introduction to the island's culinary heritage.

5. Hatzinikolaou Winery

Hatzinikolaou Winery, founded by a Greek-Australian immigrant, is known for reviving the ancient grape variety "Black Lady" (Mavrothyliko). The winery offers tours that include a walk through the vineyards, a visit to the production facilities, and tastings of their unique wines. The winery's commitment to preserving traditional grape varieties and producing high-quality wines makes it a fascinating destination for wine enthusiasts.

These tours and tastings provide a wonderful opportunity to explore the rich culinary traditions of Kos Island. If you're a wine connoisseur or an olive oil aficionado, you'll find plenty to enjoy and discover.

Chapter 8. Culture and Traditions

- Festivals and Celebrations

Kos Island is known not only for its stunning beaches and ancient history but also for its vibrant traditional festivals and events. These celebrations are deeply rooted in the island's culture, offering visitors a chance to experience the local way of life, customs, music, dance, and cuisine. Attending one of these festivals is a unique opportunity to immerse yourself in the authentic spirit of Kos.

1. Hippokrateia Festival

The Hippokrateia Festival is the most significant cultural event on Kos, running from July to September. This festival honors Hippocrates, the father of medicine, who was born on the island. The festival features a diverse range of activities, including concerts, theatrical performances, and ancient Greek tragedies. Folklore exhibitions showcase traditional crafts and customs, while sculpture workshops allow participants to engage in creative activities. Traditional dances and children's activities add to the festive atmosphere. The festival not only celebrates the island's historical connection to Hippocrates but also promotes cultural heritage and community spirit, attracting visitors from around the world.

2. Wine Festival (Mastichari)

Held every August in the charming village of Mastichari, the Wine Festival is a celebration of Kos's rich winemaking tradition. Visitors can enjoy free tastings of local wines, which are known for their unique flavors and high quality. The festival also features an array of local delicacies, allowing guests to sample traditional dishes that pair perfectly with the wines. Traditional music and dancing create a lively and welcoming atmosphere, making it a great way to experience the island's culture and hospitality. The Wine Festival is a must-visit for wine enthusiasts and those looking to immerse themselves in local traditions.

3. Honey Festival (Antimachia)

The Honey Festival in Antimachia takes place on the first Saturday after August 15th and is a sweet celebration of the island's beekeeping heritage. This festival showcases the exquisite honey produced on Kos, with various honey-based sweets and treats available for tasting. Visitors can learn about the beekeeping process and the importance of honey in local cuisine. The festival also features traditional music, dancing, and other cultural activities, making it a fun and educational experience for all ages. The Honey Festival is a delightful way to explore the island's agricultural traditions and enjoy some delicious local products.

4. Fish Festival (Kefalos)

The Fish Festival in Kefalos is celebrated twice, once in the first half of August and again in early September, as part of the greater Hippokrateia festivities. This festival highlights the island's rich maritime heritage and the importance of fishing to the local economy. Fresh fish tastings are a highlight, with a variety of seafood dishes prepared by local chefs. Traditional music and dancing add to the festive atmosphere, creating a lively and enjoyable event for visitors. The Fish Festival is a great opportunity to sample the island's seafood and experience the vibrant local culture.

5. Carnival (Antimachia and Kefalos)

Carnival in Kos is a vibrant and colorful celebration, particularly in the villages of Antimachia and Kefalos. Held on Carnival Sunday, the festivities include locals dressing up in elaborate costumes and painting their faces. Parades through the villages feature lively music, dancing, and various performances, creating a festive and joyful atmosphere. The Carnival celebrations are deeply rooted in local traditions and offer a unique glimpse into the island's cultural heritage. It's a time for the community to come together and celebrate with laughter, music, and dance, making it a memorable experience for both locals and visitors.

6. Feast of Agios Georgios (Pyli)

The Feast of Agios Georgios, celebrated in April in the village of Pyli, is a unique event that combines religious observance with local customs. The highlight of the festival is the traditional horse races, which attract participants and spectators from across the island. The event begins with a church service in honor of Saint George, followed by a procession through the village. The horse races take place in a nearby field, with riders showcasing their skills and competing for prizes. The festival also features traditional music, dancing, and feasting, creating a lively and festive atmosphere.

7. Dormition of the Virgin Mary (Antimachia and Kefalos)

The Dormition of the Virgin Mary, celebrated in August, is one of the most important religious festivals on Kos. The villages of Antimachia and Kefalos host significant festivities, including religious ceremonies, processions, and community gatherings. The celebrations begin with a church service, followed by a procession through the village streets. Traditional music and dancing are integral parts of the festivities, with locals and visitors joining in the celebrations. Feasting on local dishes and delicacies is also a highlight, making this festival a wonderful opportunity to experience the island's religious and cultural traditions.

8. Feast of Agios Ioannis (Mastichari, Kardamena, and Kefalos)

The Feast of Agios Ioannis, celebrated in August, is a major religious festival in the villages of Mastichari, Kardamena, and Kefalos. The festival includes church services, processions, and community gatherings to honor Saint John. The celebrations often feature traditional music, dancing, and feasting, with locals preparing and sharing a variety of traditional dishes. The festival provides a glimpse into the island's religious customs and the strong sense of community that characterizes life on Kos. It's a time for locals and visitors to come together and celebrate with joy and reverence.

9. Hippocrates Oath Ceremony

As part of the Hippokrateia Festival, the Hippocrates Oath Ceremony is a significant event that honors the legacy of Hippocrates, the father of medicine. The ceremony involves the reading of the Hippocratic Oath, a solemn pledge taken by medical professionals. The event is held in a historic setting, often at the ancient Asklepieion, where Hippocrates is believed to have taught. The ceremony attracts medical professionals, scholars, and visitors from around the world, highlighting the enduring influence of Hippocrates on modern medicine. It's a profound and inspiring event that underscores the island's historical significance.

10. Local Panigiria (Village Festivals)

Throughout the year, various villages on Kos host local panigiria, or village festivals, to honor their patron saints. These festivals are vibrant celebrations that include religious services, traditional music, dancing, and feasting. Each village has its own unique customs and traditions, making every panigiri a distinct experience. The festivals provide an opportunity for locals and visitors to come together and celebrate the island's rich cultural heritage. The lively atmosphere, delicious food, and warm hospitality make these village festivals a highlight of life on Kos, offering a true taste of the island's community spirit.

Attending traditional festivals and events on Kos is a fantastic way to immerse yourself in the local culture and experience the island's lively atmosphere. Whether you're witnessing a religious procession, dancing at a village festival, or sampling local wine and honey, these celebrations offer an authentic taste of the island's heritage and traditions. Make sure to time your visit to coincide with one of these festivals to enrich your Kos experience.

- Local Crafts and Souvenirs

Kos Island offers a variety of local crafts and souvenirs that reflect its rich cultural heritage and artisanal traditions.

1. Handmade Pottery

Kos is known for its beautiful handmade pottery, which includes a range of items such as vases, plates, and decorative pieces. Local artisans use traditional techniques passed down through generations to create these unique pieces. The pottery often features intricate designs and vibrant colors inspired by the island's natural beauty and ancient history. These items make for wonderful souvenirs and gifts, offering a tangible connection to the island's artistic heritage.

2. Olive Wood Products

Olive wood products are a popular souvenir from Kos, reflecting the island's abundant olive groves. Artisans craft a variety of items from this durable and beautifully grained wood, including kitchen utensils, bowls, cutting boards, and decorative pieces. Each item is unique, showcasing the natural patterns of the wood. Olive wood products are not only practical but also serve as a reminder of the island's rich agricultural traditions.

3. Traditional Textiles

Traditional textiles from Kos include handwoven fabrics, embroidered linens, and lacework. These items are often made using techniques that have been preserved for centuries. You can find beautiful tablecloths, napkins, and clothing items that feature intricate patterns and vibrant colors. These textiles make for elegant and meaningful souvenirs, representing the island's cultural heritage and the skill of its artisans.

4. Local Jewelry

Kos is home to many talented jewelers who create stunning pieces using a variety of materials, including silver, gold, and semi-precious stones. Traditional designs often incorporate motifs inspired by ancient Greek art and mythology. You can find a wide range of jewelry, from delicate necklaces and bracelets to bold statement pieces. Local jewelry makes for a special and personal souvenir, capturing the essence of the island's artistic spirit.

5. Natural Cosmetics

Natural cosmetics made from local ingredients are a popular choice for souvenirs. These products often feature olive oil, honey, and herbs, which are known for their beneficial properties. You can find a variety of items, including soaps, lotions, and skincare products, all made using traditional recipes. These natural cosmetics offer a luxurious way to take a piece of Kos's natural beauty home with you.

- Music and Dance

Music and dance play a significant role in the cultural life of Kos Island, offering visitors a chance to witness the rich heritage of Greek traditions while enjoying the island's festive atmosphere. From ancient times to the present day, music and dance have been deeply intertwined with local celebrations, religious events, and community gatherings. Exploring the island's musical and dance traditions gives visitors insight into the islanders' values, history, and spirit.

1. Traditional Greek Music on Kos

Greek music on Kos is heavily influenced by both its ancient past and its proximity to the Aegean and Dodecanese regions. Traditional Greek instruments such as the bouzouki (a stringed instrument), lyra (a small bowed instrument), laouto (a lute), and clarinet are central to the island's folk music.

Dimotiki Mousiki (folk music) is commonly played at festivals, weddings, and village gatherings, often accompanying traditional dances. The music is rhythmic and expressive, reflecting the emotions and stories of the local people. It can range from lively tunes for joyful occasions to slow, melancholic melodies that tell tales of love and hardship.

- Island Sounds: The music of Kos is also influenced by the island's maritime history, with songs of the sea and nature, especially in coastal towns like Kardamena and Kefalos.

2. Traditional Dances of Kos

Greek dance is a central element of cultural expression on the island, often performed during festivals, weddings, and other celebrations. There are a variety of traditional dances on Kos, most of which are shared with the neighboring Dodecanese islands.

- Syrtos: One of the most popular dances in Kos and across Greece, the Syrtos is a chain dance performed in a circle. The steps are graceful, and dancers often hold hands or use handkerchiefs to stay connected. This dance is traditionally performed at festivals and weddings.

- Kalamatianos: Another iconic dance, the Kalamatianos is a fast-paced version of the Syrtos, featuring 12 steps that correspond with the rhythm of the music. Dancers form a circle, and the leader often improvises more complicated moves. It's a dance of celebration, full of energy and joy.

- Sousta: Sousta is a lively couple's dance performed during celebrations. The dancers, often in pairs, face each other and simulate movements that suggest courtship. This dynamic and flirtatious dance is popular at festivals and local weddings.

- Ikariotikos: This dance, originating from the nearby island of Ikaria, is also performed on Kos, particularly in more traditional and rural villages. It starts with slow, deliberate steps but gradually speeds up, becoming a fast and energetic dance.

3. Cultural Performances and Festivals

Several festivals on Kos are centered around music and dance, allowing visitors to experience these traditions firsthand. Many of the local festivals feature live music performances accompanied by traditional dances performed by both locals and professional dance groups.

- Hippocratia Festival: As part of Kos' major summer cultural festival, the Hippocratia Festival, local musicians and dance troupes perform traditional music and dances in open-air theaters and town squares. This festival is a wonderful opportunity to experience authentic performances under the stars.

- Village Festivals: During summer, village festivals (known as Panigiria) are hosted across the island to honor local saints. These religious feasts are followed by all-night celebrations filled with traditional music, dancing, and feasting. One of the best examples is the Panagia Festival in Kefalos, where folk dancers perform for the local community and visitors.

- Local Taverna Nights: Many tavernas and restaurants, especially in tourist areas like Kos Town, Zia, and Kardamena, host Greek nights where live music and dance are featured. Guests are often invited to join in the dancing, making it an interactive experience. Bouzouki music is particularly popular, along with renditions of popular Greek songs and island folk tunes.

4. Modern Music Scene
While Kos maintains its traditional music heritage, the island also embraces modern music, particularly in the

more touristic areas. Kos Town and resort towns like Kardamena offer a lively nightlife scene, with clubs and bars playing a mix of Greek pop music (Laïko) and international hits.

- Nightclubs and Bars: The modern music scene is especially vibrant during the summer months, with Kos attracting many international DJs and artists. For those looking for a different vibe, beach bars and cafes often feature live acoustic sets, offering a more relaxed atmosphere to enjoy modern Greek and international tunes.

5. Musical Instruments of Kos
Kos shares many traditional Greek instruments with the rest of the country, and these instruments are integral to the island's music:

- Bouzouki: A long-necked string instrument resembling a mandolin, the bouzouki is key to Greek music and produces a sharp, melodic sound. It is often used in folk music and Rebetiko, a genre often called the "Greek blues."

- Lyra: A small, three-stringed instrument, the lyra is played with a bow and is a mainstay in many traditional performances. Its sound is emotive and used to accompany slow, rhythmic dances.

- Laouto: Similar to a lute, the laouto is another stringed instrument commonly played in the Dodecanese islands. Its deep, resonant sound complements the bouzouki in musical ensembles.

- Doumbek: A goblet-shaped hand drum used to keep the rhythm in traditional Greek music. Its beats are essential in creating the rhythm for dances like Syrtos and Sousta.

6. Dance Schools and Workshops
For visitors interested in learning more about Greek dance, some villages and cultural centers on Kos offer workshops during the summer. These are often organized during festivals or as part of cultural programs to teach

visitors the basic steps of traditional Greek dances. Kos' hospitality extends to sharing its music and dance traditions, making these experiences a fun and interactive way to engage with the island's culture.

Final Thoughts

Music and dance on Kos Island offer a window into the soul of its people. Whether it's the rhythmic steps of the Syrtos, the joyful melodies of the bouzouki, or the festive atmosphere of a village Panigiria, the traditions of Kos come alive through music and dance.

- Kos Folklore and Myths

Kos Island, rich in history and culture, is steeped in fascinating folklore and myths that reveal the island's deep connection to the ancient world, its gods, and the natural environment. Like many of the Greek islands, Kos has its own set of stories that have been passed down through generations, blending mythology, history, and local beliefs into captivating tales. These stories not only provide insight into the island's past but also shape its cultural identity today.

1. The Birthplace of Hippocrates and Healing Myths

Perhaps the most famous figure associated with Kos is Hippocrates, the father of modern medicine. According to tradition, Hippocrates was born on Kos around 460 BC and founded one of the first schools of medicine there. His connection to the island is not just historical but also rooted in myths that elevate his role to that of a mythical healer.

- The Plane Tree of Hippocrates: Legend has it that under a massive plane tree in Kos Town, Hippocrates taught his students the art of healing. This tree, still standing today (though likely a descendant of the original), is considered a sacred symbol of medical knowledge and is visited by tourists and medical professionals from around the world. The myth surrounding Hippocrates suggests he was more than just a man of science; he was seen as a healer with almost divine powers, carrying the blessings of the gods to cure illnesses.

- The Temple of Asclepius: In ancient times, the Asclepion of Kos was a sanctuary dedicated to Asclepius, the god of healing, and was believed to be a place where miraculous cures took place. Pilgrims from all over Greece would visit this site to seek healing through the divine intervention of Asclepius. The blending of medical practices and religious rituals in this myth underscores the belief that the gods played a central role in human health and wellbeing.

2. The Myth of Hercules on Kos

Kos plays a significant role in the mythological adventures of **Hercules** (Herakles). One of the island's most enduring myths involves Hercules landing on Kos after a storm during one of his famous voyages.

- Hercules' Struggle with the Meropes: According to legend, Hercules was shipwrecked off the coast of Kos and encountered the island's inhabitants, known as the

Meropes. The king of Kos, Eurypylus, saw Hercules as a threat and captured him. However, Hercules, renowned for his strength and wit, broke free from his captors. The myth tells of a fierce battle between Hercules and the Meropes before he was eventually freed. This story is symbolic of the island's fierce spirit and its mythological ties to the wider Greek pantheon.

- Hercules and Chalciope: Another part of the myth recounts how Hercules fell in love with Chalciope, the daughter of Eurypylus, and married her after his release. This myth not only connects Kos to the exploits of Hercules but also highlights the island's place in the wider tapestry of Greek mythology.

3. Kos and the Sea

As an island in the Aegean Sea, Kos has many myths related to the sea and its deities, particularly Poseidon, the god of the sea, and other sea creatures.

- Poseidon's Wrath: One local myth speaks of Poseidon's anger toward the inhabitants of Kos, who failed to honor him properly. According to legend, Poseidon sent massive storms and tidal waves to the island, threatening to destroy it. The people of Kos quickly built temples in his honor and performed sacrifices to appease the god, after which the storms subsided. This myth reflects the islanders' reverence for the sea and the belief that natural forces were governed by the moods of the gods.

- The Nereids: Another common myth involves the Nereids, sea nymphs who were believed to live in the waters surrounding Kos. These beautiful, mystical creatures were said to help sailors during storms, guiding them to safety. Many fishermen and sailors would offer gifts to the Nereids in return for safe passage through the treacherous waters.

4. The Giants of Kos

Greek mythology often tells of battles between gods, titans, and giants, and Kos has its own share of these epic tales. One of the island's myths centers around the Gigantomachy, the legendary war between the Olympian gods and the giants.

- The Birth of Giants: According to myth, the giants were born from the blood of Uranus (the sky god) after he was castrated by his son Cronus. The blood dripped onto the earth, and from it, the giants were born. Kos was believed to be one of the sites where these giants emerged. Local legends say that after the giants were defeated by the gods, their bodies formed the islands of the Aegean, including Kos. This myth connects the physical landscape of Kos to the divine, suggesting that the island itself is born from the struggles of ancient gods and giants.

- The Giant Polybotes: Another version of the myth tells of the giant Polybotes, who fled to Kos during the Gigantomachy. The sea god Poseidon pursued him and, in a fit of rage, broke off a part of Kos to crush him. The fragment of land became the nearby island of Nisyros, which, according to legend, is still shaking from the giant's movements beneath it. This tale serves as a reminder of the gods' power and the idea that even the landscape of the Aegean is shaped by mythological battles.

5. Local Folklore and Superstitions
Beyond ancient myths, Kos has its own local folklore and superstitions that have been passed down through generations. These stories often revolve around the mysterious and the supernatural, providing a glimpse into the everyday beliefs of the islanders.

- The Kallikantzaroi: Like many Greek islands, Kos has tales of the Kallikantzaroi, mischievous goblin-like creatures that are believed to emerge during the Twelve Days of Christmas (from Christmas to Epiphany). According to local folklore, these creatures would come out at night to cause trouble, such as spoiling food or breaking things in homes. To ward them off, locals would burn incense or hang crosses in their homes.

- The Evil Eye: The belief in the evil eye (or mati) is widespread in Greek culture, including on Kos. Islanders believe that jealousy or envy can cause harm through the evil eye, leading to misfortune or illness. To protect themselves, people wear blue glass beads or pendants in the shape of an eye, which are said to deflect the negative energy.

- Folkloric Creatures: In Kos, there are also stories of creatures like Drakoi (dragons) and nymphs that inhabit the island's forests and springs. These creatures are believed to be both protectors and tricksters, depending on how they are treated by humans.

6. Kos and Its Saints

In addition to its ancient myths, Kos is home to several important saints and religious figures whose stories are central to the island's identity.

- Saint Christodoulos: One of the most revered saints on Kos is Saint Christodoulos, who founded the famous Monastery of Saint John the Theologian on the nearby island of Patmos. Though he spent much of his life on Patmos, his connection to Kos is celebrated during religious festivals, with processions and prayers in his honor.

Final Thoughts

The folklore and myths of Kos offer a rich tapestry of stories that connect the island to both the divine and the everyday lives of its people. From the legendary feats of Hercules to the healing powers of Hippocrates and the mischievous Kallikantzaroi, these tales continue to be woven into the cultural fabric of the island. For visitors, exploring the myths and folklore of Kos is a way to experience the island's deep-rooted history and its enduring connection to the ancient world.

Chapter 9. Practical Information

- Health and Safety Tips

When visiting Kos Island, ensuring your health and safety is crucial for a memorable and worry-free vacation. By following these health and safety tips, you can make the most of your trip while staying safe and protected.

1. Stay Hydrated

Kos enjoys a Mediterranean climate, with hot and sunny summers. To avoid dehydration, it's essential to drink plenty of water throughout the day, especially when engaging in outdoor activities such as hiking, beach outings, or sightseeing. Carry a reusable water bottle with you to stay hydrated and contribute to reducing plastic waste.

2. Sun Protection

The strong sun in Kos can cause sunburn or heat-related illnesses if you aren't prepared. Make sure to:

- Apply sunscreen with a high SPF regularly, particularly after swimming.
- Wear protective clothing such as a wide-brimmed hat, sunglasses, and lightweight, breathable clothing that covers exposed skin.
- Seek shade during peak sunlight hours (typically between 11 a.m. and 3 p.m.).

3. Insect Protection

In Kos, especially during the warmer months, mosquitoes and other insects can be a nuisance. Protect yourself by:

- Using insect repellent, particularly in the evening or in more rural areas.
- Sleeping in accommodations with screens on windows or using mosquito nets when necessary.
- Wearing long sleeves and pants during dusk and dawn when mosquitoes are most active.

4. Food and Water Safety

The food in Kos is generally safe, but it's always good to take precautions when dining or drinking:

- Stick to bottled water if you're unsure about the local tap water quality, especially in more remote areas of the island.

- Ensure that food is thoroughly cooked and hot when served.

- Be cautious with raw or undercooked seafood, particularly if you have a sensitive stomach.

5. Swimming Safety

The beaches of Kos are beautiful, but the sea can present hazards if you're not careful. When swimming:

- Always pay attention to any posted signs or warnings regarding water conditions.

- Swim in designated areas that have lifeguards.

- Be cautious of strong currents or waves, particularly on windy days.

- Avoid swimming alone, and if you're not a confident swimmer, stay close to the shore.

6. Traffic and Road Safety

If you're planning to rent a car, motorbike, or quad bike on Kos, be aware of the local traffic rules and road conditions:

- Drive defensively, as some roads can be narrow, winding, and shared with pedestrians or cyclists.
- Always wear a helmet when riding a motorbike or quad bike.
- Ensure your vehicle is in good condition before setting off, particularly if you're venturing into rural or mountainous areas.
- Be cautious on gravel roads, which may be slippery or uneven.
- Follow the speed limits, and avoid distractions while driving.

7. Hiking Safety

Kos is known for its beautiful hiking trails, especially in the Dikeos Mountains. If you plan on exploring these trails:

- Wear sturdy, comfortable hiking shoes with good grip.

- Carry a map or use a GPS to navigate, as some trails may not be well-marked.
- Pack essentials such as water, snacks, a hat, sunscreen, and a first-aid kit.
- Inform someone of your hiking plans, especially if you're going to remote areas.
- Avoid hiking alone or after dark.

8. Wildlife and Plants

Kos is home to a variety of wildlife and plant species. While the island is generally safe, you should still take precautions:
- Avoid touching or approaching wild animals, especially snakes or unfamiliar insects.
- Be aware of prickly plants or thorny bushes when hiking or exploring nature trails.
- If bitten or stung, seek medical attention if the reaction is severe or if you're unsure about the nature of the injury.

9. Pharmacies and Medical Assistance

In the event of illness or injury, Kos has numerous pharmacies and healthcare facilities. Some important tips include:

- Pharmacies are well-stocked, and pharmacists can offer advice or over-the-counter medications for minor issues.

- If you need medical assistance, there are healthcare centers and hospitals in Kos Town and other parts of the island.

- It's a good idea to carry a small first-aid kit with essentials such as bandages, antiseptics, and pain relievers.

- Keep a copy of your travel insurance information and emergency contact numbers on hand in case of a serious health issue.

10. Respecting Local Laws and Customs

Staying safe also means respecting the local laws and customs of Kos:

- Avoid excessive alcohol consumption, especially when swimming or operating vehicles.

- Public displays of intoxication or disruptive behavior can lead to legal issues.
- When visiting churches or religious sites, dress modestly and behave respectfully.
- Be mindful of littering and protect the natural beauty of the island by disposing of waste properly.

By taking these precautions, you'll ensure that your trip to Kos is safe and enjoyable, allowing you to fully appreciate everything this beautiful island has to offer.

- Currency, Banking, and ATMs

Currency

The official currency of Kos, like the rest of Greece, is the Euro (€). Euro coins come in denominations of 1, 2, 5, 10, 20, and 50 cents, as well as €1 and €2. Euro banknotes are available in denominations of 5, 10, 20, 50, 100, 200, and 500 euros. The Euro is widely accepted across the island, and you can use it for all transactions, from dining and shopping to transportation and accommodation.

Banking

Kos has several banks that offer a range of services, including currency exchange, cash withdrawals, and financial advice. Major banks on the island include Piraeus Bank, Alpha Bank, and Eurobank. These banks typically operate from Monday to Friday, 8:00 AM to 2:00 PM, and are closed on weekends and public holidays. It's advisable to carry some cash, especially when visiting smaller villages or remote areas, as not all establishments accept credit or debit cards.

ATMs

ATMs are widely available across Kos, particularly in tourist areas such as Kos Town, Kardamena, and Tigaki. Most ATMs accept international cards, including Visa, MasterCard, and Maestro. It's a good idea to check with your bank about any fees for international withdrawals before you travel. ATMs usually dispense cash in euros, and you can choose from various denominations. Be aware that some ATMs may have withdrawal limits, so plan accordingly.

Currency Exchange

Currency exchange services are available at banks, exchange offices, and some hotels. The exchange rates can vary, so it's worth shopping around to get the best rate. Banks generally offer competitive rates, but they may charge a commission. Exchange offices in tourist areas might offer more convenient hours but could have less favorable rates. It's also possible to exchange currency at Kos Island International Airport (KGS), where you'll find currency exchange counters and ATMs.

Tips for Managing Money in Kos

1. Carry Cash: While credit and debit cards are widely accepted, it's always good to have some cash on hand for small purchases, tips, and in case you visit places that don't accept cards.

2. Notify Your Bank: Inform your bank of your travel plans to avoid any issues with your cards being blocked for suspicious activity.

3. Check Fees: Be aware of any foreign transaction fees your bank may charge for using your card abroad. Some

banks offer travel-friendly accounts with no foreign transaction fees.

4. Use ATMs Wisely: To minimize fees, withdraw larger amounts of cash less frequently rather than making multiple small withdrawals.

5. Keep Receipts: Save your receipts for currency exchange and ATM withdrawals in case you need to verify transactions later.

By following these tips and being aware of the available banking and currency exchange services, you can manage your money effectively and enjoy a hassle-free trip to Kos.

- Communication and Language

When visiting Kos Island, understanding the local language and communication norms can enhance your travel experience. While Greek is the official language, Kos is a popular tourist destination, and many locals speak English and other European languages.

1. Greek Language Basics

Greek is the primary language spoken on the island, and while you don't need to be fluent, learning a few basic phrases can go a long way in showing respect for the local culture. Some useful phrases include:

- - Kalimera (καλημέρα) – Good morning
- - Kalispera (καλησπέρα) – Good evening
- - Efharisto (ευχαριστώ) – Thank you
- - Parakalo (παρακαλώ) – Please/You're welcome
- - Poso kanei? (Πόσο κάνει;) – How much does it cost?
- - Ne (Ναι) – Yes
- - Ohi (Όχι) – No
- - Milate Anglika? (Μιλάτε Αγγλικά;) – Do you speak English?
- Hello: Γειά σου (Yia sou)
- Goodbye: Αντίο (Adio)
- Excuse me/Sorry: Συγγνώμη (Signomi)
- Where is…?: Πού είναι…? (Pou ine…?)

While many people in Kos, especially in tourist areas, speak English, attempting to communicate in Greek is often appreciated and can foster positive interactions.

2. English and Other Languages

Due to the island's popularity with international tourists, English is widely spoken, particularly in hotels, restaurants, shops, and tourist attractions. You will find that most service staff and business owners have a good command of English, making it easy for travelers to communicate.

In addition to English, many locals also speak German, Italian, and French, reflecting the diverse range of visitors to Kos. Signs and menus in tourist areas are often available in multiple languages, ensuring that visitors from various countries can navigate easily.

3. Non-Verbal Communication

Greek culture places a significant emphasis on non-verbal communication, so understanding body language can help you connect with locals. Key non-verbal gestures to be aware of include:

- - Nodding and Shaking the Head: In Greece, a nod upwards can mean "no," while a downward nod signifies "yes." This is the opposite of what many tourists may be used to, so it's important to clarify responses when necessary.
- - Hand Gestures: Waving with an open palm in someone's face can be considered rude, so it's best to avoid it. Instead, a more discreet hand wave or gesture is appropriate when saying hello or goodbye.
- - Personal Space: Greeks tend to stand a bit closer than people from some other cultures, especially in friendly conversations. However, maintaining polite respect for personal space is always appreciated.

4. Respecting Greek Customs in Communication

When interacting with locals in Kos, showing respect for their cultural communication norms will make your experience more enjoyable:

- - Politeness: Greeks appreciate politeness and courtesy, so always greet people with a smile and a friendly tone. Using "please" and "thank you" (in Greek, if possible) shows respect.
- - Eye Contact: Direct eye contact is considered a sign of honesty and engagement. When speaking with someone, maintaining eye contact conveys that you are interested and involved in the conversation.
- - Volume and Tone: Greeks tend to speak in animated tones, especially during social conversations. This is not a sign of anger or impatience but a reflection of their expressive culture.

5. Signage and Public Information

In Kos, signage in tourist areas is typically bilingual, with Greek and English being the most common. Important public information such as road signs, directions, and notices in airports, bus stations, and popular attractions will generally be easy to understand for English-speaking travelers.

6. Mobile Communication

Mobile phone coverage in Kos is good, with reliable 4G networks available across most of the island. If you're planning to stay connected during your trip, consider purchasing a local SIM card or ensuring that your phone plan offers affordable international roaming.

Most cafes, restaurants, and hotels offer free Wi-Fi, so you can easily access the internet to communicate with family and friends or check online maps and travel guides.

By familiarizing yourself with basic Greek phrases and understanding the local communication customs, you'll be able to navigate Kos Island with ease and enhance your interactions with locals, enriching your travel experience.

- Travel Insurance and Emergency Contacts

When planning your trip to Kos Island, ensuring you have adequate travel insurance and are familiar with emergency contacts is essential for a safe and stress-free vacation. Travel insurance provides financial protection against unforeseen events, while knowing the appropriate emergency contacts can be a lifesaver in case of accidents or urgent situations.

1. Travel Insurance: A Must-Have

Travel insurance is a vital part of any trip, offering peace of mind in case of unexpected problems. Here are key areas where travel insurance can help you:

- Medical Coverage: This covers the cost of medical treatment, hospitalization, and emergency evacuation in case of illness or injury during your stay. Healthcare in Greece is generally good, but it can be costly for travelers without insurance.

- Trip Cancellation/Interruption: If your trip is canceled or cut short due to unforeseen circumstances, such as illness, injury, or family emergencies, travel insurance can help you recover non-refundable costs for flights, hotels, and other prepaid expenses.

- Lost or Stolen Luggage: In case your luggage is lost, delayed, or stolen, travel insurance can cover the cost of replacing essential items like clothing, toiletries, and travel documents.

- Flight Delays: Insurance can also cover additional expenses incurred due to flight delays, such as meals, accommodation, and transportation.

- Accidental Damage or Theft: Many policies include coverage for theft or damage to your belongings, including electronics, cameras, or jewelry.

When purchasing travel insurance, ensure the policy covers the activities you plan to participate in, such as water sports, hiking, or diving. Double-check that it also includes emergency medical evacuation, which is crucial for remote island destinations like Kos.

2. Emergency Contacts on Kos Island

In the unlikely event that you encounter an emergency during your visit to Kos, it's essential to know the emergency contacts and local procedures. Below is a list of important numbers and resources:

- European Emergency Number: 112

  - This is the universal emergency number in Greece and across Europe. Dial 112 for immediate assistance in any type of emergency, including medical, fire, police, or accidents.

- Medical Emergency: 166

  - For urgent medical assistance, such as serious injuries, accidents, or life-threatening conditions, dial 166 for an ambulance.

- Police: 100

- In case of theft, assault, or other legal emergencies, dial 100 to contact the local police.

- Fire Department: 199
 - If you encounter a fire or need assistance with fire-related emergencies, contact the fire department by dialing 199.

- Tourist Police: 22420 23333
 - Kos has a tourist police force dedicated to helping visitors with issues such as theft, scams, or legal concerns. They are often better equipped to handle problems specific to tourists and can communicate in several languages.

- Hospitals and Medical Centers
 - Kos General Hospital: +30 22420 23031 / 24451
  - The main hospital in Kos Town provides general medical care and emergency services.
  - Private Medical Centers: There are also private medical clinics and healthcare providers that cater to

tourists, offering quicker services for non-life-threatening conditions.

3. Pharmacies and First Aid

Pharmacies are abundant on Kos Island, particularly in Kos Town and other tourist-heavy areas. Pharmacists in Greece are highly trained and can provide medications and advice for minor ailments without the need for a doctor's prescription.

- Pharmacy Hours: Pharmacies in tourist areas usually operate throughout the day, but in smaller villages, hours may vary. In case of a medical emergency after hours, there's always an emergency pharmacy open—look for the posted list at the door of any pharmacy, which will include the nearest one that is open after hours.

4. Consular Assistance

If you're a foreign national visiting Kos and find yourself in need of consular assistance—such as in cases of lost passports, legal trouble, or major emergencies—it's crucial to have the contact information of your country's embassy or consulate in Greece. Most embassies are located in Athens, but they provide support for citizens throughout the country, including the islands.

- Embassies in Greece: Look up your country's embassy or consulate contact information before your trip. Many embassies provide 24/7 assistance hotlines in case of emergencies.

5. Tips for Staying Safe on Kos Island

To avoid unnecessary risks and ensure a safe trip, here are a few additional safety tips:

- Stay Informed: Keep track of local news and weather forecasts, especially if you're planning outdoor activities like hiking or water sports.
- Keep Valuables Safe: While Kos is generally safe, petty theft can occur, especially in crowded tourist areas. Keep valuables in a secure location and be cautious with your belongings in busy areas.

- Know Your Location: Familiarize yourself with the layout of your hotel or accommodation, including exits and safety procedures. Know the location of the nearest hospital or clinic.
- Keep Emergency Numbers Handy: Store the essential emergency numbers in your phone, and write them down in case your phone runs out of battery.

By taking the proper precautions, purchasing travel insurance, and knowing the local emergency contacts, you can enjoy a safe and pleasant visit to Kos Island, confident that you're prepared for any situation.

Chapter 10. Day Trips and Nearby Islands

- Nisyros Island

A day trip from Kos to Nisyros Island offers a perfect opportunity to explore one of the most unique and captivating islands in the Dodecanese. Known for its volcanic landscapes, picturesque villages, and laid-back atmosphere, Nisyros is a hidden gem that invites visitors to experience both adventure and tranquility in a single day.

1. Getting to Nisyros from Kos

The journey to Nisyros from Kos is straightforward, and you can take a ferry or organized boat trip from Kardamena on Kos. The ferry ride takes around 50 minutes and offers stunning views of the Aegean Sea and neighboring islands along the way. Ferry services usually operate several times a day, especially during the summer months.

- Ferry or Boat Tour: Depending on your preference, you can either book a standard ferry ticket or join a guided boat tour that includes additional amenities like onboard commentary and organized excursions upon arrival.
- Departure Points: Most ferries and tours to Nisyros depart from Kardamena, so if you're staying in other parts of Kos, you may need to arrange transportation to the port.

2. Exploring Mandraki: The Charming Harbor Town
Upon arrival in Nisyros, you'll dock in Mandraki, the island's main town. Mandraki is a picturesque harbor town filled with whitewashed houses, narrow alleyways, and vibrant flowers. It's a great place to start your day trip, offering opportunities for sightseeing, shopping, and dining.

- Visit the Monastery of Panagia Spiliani: Perched on a hill above Mandraki, this monastery is a peaceful sanctuary with a stunning panoramic view of the island.

The monastery is dedicated to the Virgin Mary and holds significant religious importance.

- Stroll Through the Narrow Streets: Wander through the charming streets of Mandraki, where you'll find local shops selling handmade crafts, pottery, and traditional foods.

3. Discover the Nisyros Volcano

The highlight of any visit to Nisyros is the volcano, which is one of the most famous active volcanoes in Greece. Located in the Stefanos Crater, this natural wonder offers a rare opportunity to walk inside a caldera and experience the lunar-like landscape.

- Stefanos Crater: The crater is massive, with steaming vents and a strong sulfur smell. You can walk down into the crater and see the bubbling hot springs up close, giving you a surreal, out-of-this-world experience.
- Volcanological Museum: For a deeper understanding of the island's volcanic history, stop by the Volcanological Museum in the village of Nikia. It provides insights into

the geology of Nisyros and other volcanic regions in Greece.

4. Explore Traditional Villages
Nisyros is dotted with traditional villages that retain their authentic charm, each offering a glimpse into the island's rich culture and history.

- Nikia: Located on the edge of the volcanic caldera, Nikia is known for its beautiful square, traditional houses, and breathtaking views of the volcano and the Aegean Sea. The village is quiet and peaceful, making it perfect for a relaxing walk.
- Emporios: Another picturesque village, Emporios, is built into the mountainside and offers stunning views of the island and sea. It is also home to hot springs, which have been used for centuries for their therapeutic properties.

5. Lunch and Local Cuisine
After exploring, you'll likely want to enjoy a delicious meal featuring the local cuisine of Nisyros. Traditional

Greek tavernas in Mandraki and the surrounding villages serve fresh seafood, local cheeses, and dishes flavored with the island's herbs and spices.

- Local Specialties: Try dishes like pitaridia (homemade pasta), kapamas (goat stuffed with rice and herbs), and fresh seafood such as grilled octopus or fried calamari. Don't forget to sample the local soumada, a traditional almond-flavored drink.
- Seaside Dining: For a truly relaxing experience, enjoy lunch at a seaside taverna in Mandraki, where you can dine with views of the sea and watch the fishing boats come in.

6. Relax at the Thermal Springs

Nisyros is known for its natural hot springs, which are believed to have healing properties. If time permits, head to the Loutra Thermal Springs near Mandraki, where you can take a dip in the warm, mineral-rich waters. It's the perfect way to relax and rejuvenate after a morning of exploration.

7. Return to Kos

After a day of exploring Nisyros, you'll return to Kos by ferry or boat in the late afternoon or early evening. Be sure to check the ferry schedule in advance to ensure a smooth return trip.

8. Tips for a Successful Day Trip

- Wear Comfortable Shoes: Exploring the crater, villages, and narrow streets of Nisyros involves a lot of walking, so comfortable shoes are a must.
- Sun Protection: The Greek sun can be intense, especially during summer, so bring sunscreen, a hat, and sunglasses to protect yourself from sunburn.
- Hydration: Be sure to carry water with you, especially if you're visiting the volcano, where it can get quite hot and dry.
- Cash: Some smaller shops and tavernas in Nisyros may not accept credit cards, so it's a good idea to have some cash on hand for purchases and meals.

A day trip from Kos to Nisyros Island is a memorable experience that offers a perfect balance of natural beauty, history, and relaxation. From the volcanic crater to the charming villages, every part of the island invites you to explore its hidden treasures and enjoy the serene atmosphere that sets Nisyros apart from other destinations in the Dodecanese.

- Kalymnos Island

A day trip from Kos to Kalymnos Island offers an opportunity to discover the authentic charm of one of the most intriguing islands in the Dodecanese. Known as the "Sponge Divers' Island," Kalymnos is famous for its deep-rooted traditions in sponge diving, its stunning mountainous landscapes, crystal-clear waters, and vibrant rock climbing scene.

1. Getting to Kalymnos from Kos
The journey from Kos to Kalymnos is easy and scenic, with ferries and boats regularly making the trip between the two islands.

- Ferry Options: Ferries to Kalymnos generally depart from Mastichari in Kos, and the journey takes about 30 to 45 minutes. During the summer months, there are multiple departures daily, so it's easy to plan a day trip.
- Organized Boat Tours: You can also book an organized boat tour that includes stops at various attractions on Kalymnos, often with additional activities like snorkeling or visiting nearby islets such as Pserimos.

2. Arrival in Pothia: The Capital of Kalymnos

You will arrive in Pothia, the capital and main port of Kalymnos. Pothia is a vibrant town nestled between hills, with colorful houses built amphitheatrically around the port.

- Explore Pothia: Start your visit with a stroll through the narrow streets of Pothia, where you can admire the town's neoclassical architecture, vibrant facades, and beautiful harbor views. The town is also home to many shops and cafes where you can enjoy a coffee or a light snack.

- Sponge Diving Museum: Kalymnos is historically known for its sponge diving industry, and a visit to the Kalymnos Sponge Diving Museum offers an excellent insight into this fascinating tradition. The museum showcases the tools, techniques, and history of sponge diving that shaped the island's culture and economy.
- Monastery of Agios Savvas: For panoramic views of Pothia and the surrounding landscape, visit the Monastery of Agios Savvas, located on a hill overlooking the town. The monastery is known for its beautiful architecture and serene atmosphere.

3. Vathy: The Hidden Gem of Kalymnos

After exploring Pothia, head to Vathy, one of the island's most picturesque villages. Vathy is a lush valley with a hidden fjord-like harbor, known as Rina. It's a peaceful escape from the bustle of Pothia, with lush greenery and tranquil waters.

- Boat Ride in Rina Bay: One of the highlights of visiting Vathy is taking a boat ride around Rina Bay, where you can explore sea caves and swim in the clear blue waters. You can also rent a kayak or paddleboard to explore the bay on your own.

- Tavernas by the Water: Enjoy lunch at one of the local tavernas by the water, where you can taste fresh seafood and traditional Kalymnian dishes like mououri (slow-cooked goat with rice) and makarounes (local pasta).

4. Rock Climbing Adventures

Kalymnos is world-famous for rock climbing, and even if you're not a professional climber, it's worth exploring some of the island's climbing spots.

- Climbing Routes: Kalymnos offers more than 2,000 climbing routes of varying difficulty, attracting climbers from all over the world. If you're interested in trying it out, you can book a guided climbing session or simply hike along the well-marked trails that lead to the climbing areas.
- Climbing Villages: The villages of Massouri and Myrties are the main hubs for climbers. Even if you

don't climb, these areas offer stunning views of the sea and the island of Telendos.

5. Relaxing on Kalymnos Beaches

Kalymnos boasts beautiful beaches with crystal-clear waters, ideal for relaxing and swimming during your day trip.

- Kantouni Beach: Located near the village of Panormos, Kantouni Beach is a sandy beach with calm waters, perfect for swimming and sunbathing.
- Myrties and Massouri Beaches: These two beaches are popular for their soft sand and beautiful views of the neighboring islet of Telendos. The beaches are lined with cafes and tavernas, making them a great place to unwind.
- Platis Yialos: This beach is a bit more secluded and known for its calm waters and peaceful surroundings, ideal for those looking for a more quiet beach experience.

6. Excursion to Telendos Islet

If you have extra time during your day trip, consider taking a short boat ride from Myrties to the islet of Telendos, just a few minutes away by boat. Telendos is a tiny, car-free island with a peaceful atmosphere, perfect for a short hike or a swim at one of its pristine beaches.

7. Savor Local Delicacies

Kalymnos offers a wide range of traditional foods that reflect the island's history and seafaring culture. Don't miss the chance to sample local specialties during your trip.

- Local Dishes: Besides fresh seafood, Kalymnos is known for dishes like fouskes (sea anemones), spinialo (preserved sea urchins), and mououri.
- Sweet Treats: Try myzithra (a local cheese) and the famous Kalymnian honey, which is considered some of the best in Greece. You'll also find traditional pastries like katoumari (honey and cinnamon pie).

8. Return to Kos

After a full day of exploring Kalymnos, you'll return to Kos by ferry or boat in the late afternoon or evening. The return journey offers another chance to enjoy the scenic views of the Aegean Sea and surrounding islands.

9. Tips for a Successful Day Trip

- Plan Ahead: Check ferry schedules in advance, especially during the off-season, as they can be limited.

- Comfortable Shoes: Bring comfortable shoes for walking and exploring the island's villages and hiking trails.

- Sun Protection: Be sure to bring sunscreen, a hat, and sunglasses, as the sun can be quite strong, especially during the summer months.

- Cas: Some smaller shops and tavernas may not accept credit cards, so it's always a good idea to have some cash on hand.

- Pserimos Island

A day trip from Kos to Pserimos Island offers a peaceful retreat into a slower pace of life, far removed from the more bustling parts of the Dodecanese Islands. Located just a short boat ride away, Pserimos is an unspoiled paradise known for its tranquil beaches, crystal-clear waters, and traditional charm. With a small population of around 100 inhabitants, the island is perfect for those seeking a serene escape and a true taste of authentic Greek island life.

1. Getting to Pserimos from Kos
The journey from Kos to Pserimos is simple and convenient, with several options available.

- Ferries and Boats: Pserimos is reachable by boat from Kos, with regular departures from Mastichari and Kos Town. The trip takes about 45 minutes to an hour, depending on the type of boat.
- Organized Excursions: Many tour companies in Kos offer organized day trips to Pserimos, often as part of

island-hopping packages that also include visits to Kalymnos and Plati. These excursions typically allow for a few hours on Pserimos to explore and relax.

2. Arrival at Pserimos Harbor

Upon arrival at Pserimos Harbor, you'll immediately notice the island's laid-back atmosphere. The small port area is charming, with a handful of traditional tavernas and cafes offering fresh seafood and local specialties.

- Relaxed Atmosphere: Pserimos is free from the hustle and bustle of larger islands, making it an ideal destination for those seeking peace and quiet. The island has very few cars, and life moves at a leisurely pace.
- Welcoming Locals: The small community of Pserimos is friendly and welcoming. You can chat with the locals, many of whom are involved in fishing or agriculture, and get a real sense of island life.

3. Beaches on Pserimos

Pserimos is best known for its pristine beaches, which are perfect for sunbathing, swimming, and snorkeling.

- Main Beach (Avlakia Beach): The main beach near the harbor is a beautiful stretch of soft golden sand with shallow, crystal-clear waters. This beach is ideal for families, as the waters are calm and safe for children. The beach is relatively unspoiled, with a few tavernas nearby offering refreshments and local food.
- Other Beaches: For those who want more seclusion, there are several other small, hidden coves around the island that can be reached on foot or by boat. Vathis Bay and Tavari Beach are quieter alternatives for those who prefer a more private beach experience.

4. Exploring Pserimos

Pserimos is a small island, and much of its charm lies in its simplicity. While it doesn't have major attractions or historical landmarks, there are plenty of opportunities to explore its natural beauty and traditional way of life.

- Walking and Hiking: Pserimos is a haven for hikers and walkers. The island is crisscrossed by footpaths that lead through olive groves, past small farms, and along the coast. A popular hike takes you up to the island's hilltop for panoramic views of the Aegean Sea and neighboring islands.

- Church of Panagia: A small but lovely church dedicated to Panagia (the Virgin Mary) sits on a hill overlooking the harbor. It's worth the short walk to the top for the views alone.

5. Local Cuisine

One of the highlights of a day trip to Pserimos is indulging in traditional Greek food at one of the island's few tavernas.

- Fresh Seafood: Given its fishing heritage, Pserimos offers some of the freshest seafood in the Dodecanese. Try grilled octopus, calamari, and sardines, which are often caught the same day they're served.
- Traditional Dishes: In addition to seafood, you can enjoy classic Greek dishes such as moussaka, souvlaki, and Greek salad. Many of the tavernas also serve local specialties like fava (split pea puree) and kleftiko (slow-cooked lamb).

- Homemade Treats: Don't forget to try some of the island's homemade desserts, such as baklava and loukoumades (honey-soaked doughnuts), washed down with a shot of ouzo or tsipouro.

6. Snorkeling and Swimming

The waters around Pserimos are incredibly clear, making it an excellent spot for snorkeling and swimming.

- Snorkeling: Bring your snorkeling gear or rent some from the local shops. The underwater life is vibrant, with plenty of fish and marine creatures to spot. The rocky coves and shallow waters provide ideal conditions for exploring the underwater world.
- Swimming: The calm waters around Pserimos are perfect for swimming, whether at the main beach or in one of the more secluded coves. The lack of waves and the gentle slope of the beaches make it safe and enjoyable for all ages.

7. Peace and Serenity

One of the main draws of Pserimos is its tranquil, untouched beauty. Unlike the more developed islands of Kos and Kalymnos, Pserimos feels like a step back in time, where life moves at a slower, more traditional pace. The island has very few tourists, especially outside the high season, making it a perfect destination for those seeking peace and quiet.

8. Return to Kos

After a day of relaxation and exploration on Pserimos, you'll return to Kos by ferry or boat in the late afternoon or evening. The return trip provides a final opportunity to soak in the beauty of the Aegean Sea, with the sun setting over the horizon.

9. Tips for a Day Trip to Pserimos

- Bring Essentials: Pserimos is a small, undeveloped island, so bring along essentials like sunscreen, water, and a hat. While there are a few small shops and tavernas, options can be limited.

- Cash: Some of the island's small businesses may not accept credit cards, so it's a good idea to bring cash.

- Comfortable Footwear: If you plan on exploring the island beyond the main beach, wear comfortable shoes for walking on the island's footpaths.

- Plati Island

A day trip from Kos to Plati Island offers a unique opportunity to explore one of the most serene and unspoiled islets in the Dodecanese. Located between Kalymnos and Pserimos, Plati is a small, uninhabited island known for its crystal-clear waters, stunning underwater landscapes, and tranquil atmosphere. With no permanent residents, the island is ideal for those seeking a peaceful escape from the busier islands in the region.

1. Getting to Plati Island from Kos

While Plati is a small and remote islet, it is easily accessible as part of an organized day trip or boat tour.

- Boat Tours: Most visitors to Plati arrive via boat tours that depart from Kos, Mastichari, or Kefalos. These tours often include stops at nearby islands like Kalymnos and Pserimos, allowing for a well-rounded island-hopping experience. The boat journey typically takes about 45 minutes to 1 hour from Kos.

- Private Charters: For a more personalized experience, private boat charters are available, allowing you to explore the island and its surroundings at your own pace.

2. Exploring Plati

Plati Island is known for its wild beauty, offering stunning views, pristine waters, and a quiet atmosphere perfect for relaxation.

- Uninhabited and Untouched: Since Plati is uninhabited, it remains a peaceful and untouched destination. There are no shops, restaurants, or hotels on the island, making it a true retreat for nature lovers and those looking to escape the crowds.

- Remote Experience: Due to its small size and lack of development, Plati feels wonderfully remote. Visitors can enjoy the sense of isolation and tranquility that comes with being on a deserted island.

3. Beaches on Plati
One of the highlights of visiting Plati is the opportunity to enjoy its beautiful beaches, which are surrounded by clear, calm waters.

- Secluded Beaches: The island has a few secluded beaches where visitors can swim, sunbathe, and snorkel. The beaches are typically uncrowded, offering a sense of privacy and peacefulness.
- Crystal-Clear Waters: Plati's waters are incredibly clear, making them ideal for swimming and snorkeling. The beaches have a mix of pebbles and sand, and the sea is usually calm, creating perfect conditions for a relaxing dip.

4. Snorkeling and Diving
Plati Island is a paradise for snorkeling and diving enthusiasts, with its clear waters and rich underwater life.

- Snorkeling: The rocky coastline around Plati is home to a variety of marine species, making it an excellent spot for snorkeling. The underwater visibility is fantastic, allowing you to see fish, coral formations, and other marine life up close.

- Diving: For those interested in diving, the waters around Plati offer excellent opportunities. Some boat tours provide diving gear, allowing visitors to explore the deeper parts of the sea and discover the island's underwater beauty. The island's rocky sea bed is perfect for spotting fish and other marine creatures.

5. Landmarks on Plati

Though Plati is largely uninhabited, it does have a couple of notable landmarks that add to its charm.

- Old Chapel: On the island, you'll find a small, white-washed chapel, which stands out against the rocky landscape. While simple, this chapel adds to the tranquil atmosphere and offers a picturesque view over the sea.

It's a peaceful place to sit and reflect while enjoying the surrounding natural beauty.

- Shipwrecks: Some boat tours include a visit to an old shipwreck site near Plati, which can be viewed from the boat or while snorkeling. This adds an extra layer of interest for visitors who enjoy exploring maritime history.

6. Swimming and Sunbathing

Plati's beaches and secluded coves provide the perfect setting for a relaxing day by the sea.

- Calm Waters: The waters surrounding Plati are typically calm and warm, making them ideal for swimming. Whether you're looking to take a refreshing dip or simply float in the sea, the serene conditions make it a perfect spot.
- Sunbathing: The island's peaceful environment makes it a great place to lay out a towel and enjoy sunbathing in the middle of nature. With few visitors and no crowds, you can find a quiet spot to enjoy the sun.

7. Wildlife on Plati

Plati's lack of development means that it is home to a variety of wildlife, particularly birds.

- Birdwatching: Birdwatchers will appreciate the island's quiet environment, which attracts several species of seabirds. You may spot them nesting on the rocky cliffs or gliding over the waters.
- Marine Life: In addition to birdlife, the waters around Plati are teeming with marine creatures, from colorful fish to sea urchins and crabs. Snorkelers will have plenty to observe under the water.

8. Relaxation and Solitude

A visit to Plati Island is all about relaxation and soaking in the natural beauty of the area. The island's lack of infrastructure and its remote location make it a perfect getaway for those who want to escape the hustle and bustle of daily life.

- Disconnecting: Since there are no facilities or large crowds on Plati, it's an excellent place to disconnect from the outside world and enjoy some solitude. Whether you're lounging on the beach or exploring the island's rugged landscape, Plati offers the opportunity to unwind in a truly natural environment.

9. Tips for Visiting Plati
- Bring Essentials: As there are no shops or restaurants on Plati, be sure to bring everything you need for the day, including water, snacks, sunscreen, and a hat.
- Sun Protection: The island has little natural shade, so it's essential to bring sun protection, such as a hat, sunglasses, and plenty of sunscreen.
- Snorkeling Gear: If you plan to snorkel, bring your own equipment, as there are no rental facilities on the island. Some boat tours provide gear, but it's best to check in advance.

10. Return to Kos
After a day of sunbathing, swimming, and exploring the serene landscape of Plati, you'll return to Kos by boat in the afternoon or evening. The boat ride back is a great

opportunity to relax and reflect on the peaceful time spent on this remote island.

- Patmos Island

A day trip to **Patmos Island** from Kos offers an unforgettable experience, allowing travelers to explore one of the most spiritual and culturally significant islands in the Aegean. Known for its rich history, religious significance, and stunning natural landscapes, Patmos is an ideal destination for those interested in both relaxation and exploration.

1. Getting to Patmos from Kos

Traveling from Kos to Patmos typically involves taking a ferry or joining an organized tour, as Patmos is about 70 kilometers north of Kos.

- Ferry Routes: Several ferry services connect Kos and Patmos, with travel times ranging between 2 to 4 hours, depending on the type of ferry and the specific route. You can catch a ferry from Kos Town or Mastichari.

- Day Tours: Organized day tours are a convenient way to explore Patmos, as they include transportation and guided tours of the island's key attractions. These tours typically depart early in the morning and return in the evening.

2. Spiritual Significance of Patmos

Patmos is renowned for its deep spiritual and religious history. It is often referred to as the "Island of the Apocalypse" because it is where St. John the Theologian is believed to have written the Book of Revelation.

- Monastery of St. John the Theologian: Perched high above Chora, the capital of Patmos, the Monastery of St. John is a UNESCO World Heritage site and one of the island's main attractions. Built in 1088, this impressive monastery is home to a rich collection of religious icons, manuscripts, and relics. Visitors can tour the monastery and learn about its religious importance while taking in panoramic views of the island.
- Cave of the Apocalypse: Another must-visit site is the Cave of the Apocalypse, where St. John is said to have

received his visions. The cave has been turned into a chapel, and pilgrims from around the world visit to pay their respects and experience its spiritual ambiance.

3. Exploring Chora
Chora, the main town on Patmos, is a charming medieval settlement that offers a mix of history, culture, and stunning views.

- Whitewashed Buildings: Chora is known for its traditional whitewashed houses, narrow streets, and beautiful courtyards filled with bougainvillea. As you stroll through the town, you'll discover hidden squares, quaint chapels, and local artisan shops selling handmade crafts and religious souvenirs.
- Museums: Chora is also home to a couple of small but fascinating museums, such as the Ecclesiastical Museum, which houses religious artifacts from the monastery, and the Folklore Museum, which showcases the island's cultural heritage.

4. Skala Port

Skala is the main port of Patmos and the hub of the island's commercial activity. Most visitors arrive at Skala, where they can explore its lively harborfront, lined with cafes, restaurants, and shops.

- Harborfront Stroll: Skala's waterfront is a perfect place to start your exploration of the island. You can enjoy a leisurely walk along the harbor, watch the boats come and go, and dine at one of the local tavernas serving fresh seafood.
- Boat Trips: From Skala, you can also catch boat trips to nearby islets or take a tour of the coastline, stopping at secluded beaches and coves.

5. Beautiful Beaches

Although Patmos is best known for its religious sites, it also boasts beautiful beaches where visitors can relax and enjoy the clear waters of the Aegean Sea.

- Psili Ammos Beach: One of the most famous beaches on the island is Psili Ammos, a stunning stretch of golden sand accessible by boat or a short hike. Its secluded location and crystal-clear waters make it a favorite for sunbathers and swimmers alike.

- Agriolivado Beach: Located near Skala, Agriolivado Beach is another popular spot for visitors looking to unwind. The beach offers sunbeds and umbrellas, as well as shallow waters perfect for swimming.

- Grikos Bay: For a more tranquil beach experience, head to Grikos Bay, a peaceful cove surrounded by lush hills and dotted with fishing boats. It's an ideal place for a quiet afternoon by the sea.

6. Hiking and Nature Trails

Patmos' hilly terrain offers excellent opportunities for hiking, with trails that take you through the island's beautiful landscapes and provide breathtaking views of the sea.

- Hiking to the Monastery: One of the most popular hikes on the island is the trail from Skala to the Monastery of St. John. The walk takes about 45 minutes and offers stunning views of the surrounding countryside and coastline.

- Nature Walks: Patmos is also known for its wild, rugged nature, with several trails leading through forests, rocky hills, and coastal paths. Hiking enthusiasts will find plenty of routes to explore, each offering a different perspective of the island's beauty.

7. Local Cuisine

During your visit to Patmos, don't miss the chance to sample the island's delicious local cuisine, which is characterized by fresh seafood, traditional Greek dishes, and locally grown produce.

- Seafood Delicacies: Given its maritime location, seafood is a staple on Patmos. Dishes like grilled octopus, fresh fish, and shrimp saganaki (shrimp in a tomato and feta sauce) are commonly served in the island's tavernas.
- Local Specialties: Patmos is also known for its local specialties such as Patmian cheese pie (a savory pie

filled with a mixture of cheeses) and soumada, a traditional almond-based drink.

8. Patmos Festivals and Events
Patmos hosts several festivals and cultural events throughout the year, many of which are tied to the island's religious heritage.

- Feast of St. John the Theologian: The most important religious event on the island is the Feast of St. John, which is celebrated with processions, church services, and local festivities. It's a unique opportunity to witness the deep spiritual traditions of the island.
- International Film Festival: Patmos also hosts an annual International Film Festival every summer, attracting filmmakers and movie enthusiasts from around the world.

9. Practical Tips for Visiting Patmos
- What to Bring: Since Patmos has many religious sites, it's a good idea to dress modestly when visiting the monastery or the Cave of the Apocalypse. Bring

comfortable shoes for walking and hiking, as the island's terrain can be steep in some areas.

- Currency: Patmos uses the Euro (€), and you'll find ATMs and currency exchange services in Skala.

- Time of Visit: If you're visiting during the summer, aim to start your day trip early to avoid the heat and crowds at popular sites like the monastery and cave.

A day trip to Patmos Island offers a perfect mix of history, spirituality, and natural beauty. Whether you're drawn to the island for its religious significance, stunning beaches, or charming villages, Patmos will leave you with lasting memories and a deep appreciation for its unique character.

Chapter 11. A Perfect 3 Days Itinerary

Kos is an island rich in history, culture, and natural beauty, making it a fantastic destination for travelers looking for a mix of relaxation, exploration, and adventure. Below is a detailed 3-day itinerary designed to give you a perfect blend of experiences.

Day 1: Exploring Kos Town and Ancient History
Your first day will be spent exploring the historical heart of Kos and some of the island's most iconic landmarks.

Morning
- Kos Town Walkabout

Start your day with a leisurely breakfast in one of the cafes along Eleftherias Square, the vibrant heart of Kos Town. Here you'll enjoy views of the Mosque of Gazi Hassan Pasha and the Agora (ancient marketplace).

- Neratzia Castle

After breakfast, head to the impressive Neratzia Castle, located right by the harbor. This medieval fortress offers breathtaking views of the town and the Aegean Sea. Spend some time exploring its ancient walls and towers, imagining the island's rich history of defending against pirates and invaders.

- Hippocrates Tree & Ancient Agora

A short walk from the castle will take you to the Plane Tree of Hippocrates, said to be where the father of medicine taught his students. Nearby is the Ancient Agora, a fascinating archaeological site filled with ruins of temples, columns, and mosaics.

Lunch

- Harborfront Dining

Enjoy lunch by the harbor at one of the many seaside tavernas. You can savor traditional Greek dishes such as fresh fish, grilled calamari, and Greek salad while soaking in the views of the yachts and boats.

Afternoon

- Asclepeion

In the afternoon, take a short drive or taxi ride to the Asclepeion, the most famous ancient medical center in Greece. This sanctuary was dedicated to Asclepius, the god of healing, and is where Hippocrates practiced medicine. The site sits on a hill, offering panoramic views of the surrounding landscape and sea.

- Roman Odeon

Head back to Kos Town and visit the well-preserved Roman Odeon, an ancient theater that once hosted musical performances and gladiator fights.

Evening

- Stroll and Sunset in Zia

As the evening approaches, take a trip to the mountain village of Zia, located on the slopes of Mount Dikeos. Zia is known for its breathtaking sunsets. Wander through the narrow streets, explore local artisan shops, and grab a seat at one of the tavernas to enjoy a traditional Greek dinner while watching the sun set over the Aegean.

Day 2: Beaches and Relaxation

Day 2 is all about relaxation and enjoying the natural beauty of Kos. From golden beaches to scenic drives, this day is perfect for unwinding.

Morning

- Paradise Beach

Start your day early and head to Paradise Beach, one of the most famous beaches on the island. This long stretch of golden sand and crystal-clear waters is ideal for swimming, sunbathing, and water sports. You can rent jet skis or go paddleboarding. If you prefer a quieter spot, walk down to one of the more secluded areas of the beach.

Lunch

- Beachside Tavernas

Enjoy a laid-back lunch at one of the beachfront tavernas. Try some local favorites like souvlaki, tzatziki, and gyros, along with a chilled glass of ouzo or beer.

Afternoon

- Thermes Hot Springs

After a relaxing morning, head to Thermes, a natural hot spring located on the southeastern coast. These warm, mineral-rich waters are said to have healing properties. Relax in the hot springs while taking in the spectacular views of the sea.

- Explore Kefalos

In the late afternoon, take a scenic drive to the village of Kefalos on the southwestern tip of the island. Visit Agios Stefanos Beach, where ancient ruins sit just a short distance from the sea, and enjoy a stroll around this charming, traditional village.

Evening

- Dinner in Kefalos

Stay in Kefalos for dinner at a local taverna, where you can enjoy freshly caught seafood and traditional Kos cuisine. Psarosoupa (fish soup) and octopus stew are local delicacies to try.

Day 3: Adventure and Island Hopping

The third day is for adventure lovers and those who want to experience more of Kos's surrounding beauty.

Morning

- Cycling in Kos

Kos is famous for its flat terrain and well-maintained cycling routes. Rent a bike and explore the island's coastal paths or countryside roads. A popular cycling route is from Kos Town to Tigaki Beach, which offers stunning views and takes you through olive groves and fields.

Lunch

- Lunch in Tigaki

Once you reach Tigaki, a peaceful beach village, enjoy lunch at one of the local seaside tavernas. Try moussaka, a traditional dish made with eggplant, potatoes, and minced meat, or opt for lighter seafood options.

Afternoon

- Day Trip to Nisyros Island

In the afternoon, take a boat trip to Nisyros, a volcanic island near Kos. Visit the island's impressive crater, where you can walk inside the volcano and feel the heat rising from the earth. Explore the charming village of Mandraki with its narrow alleys, whitewashed houses, and picturesque churches.

- Island Walks

Stroll around the scenic trails of Nisyros, taking in the unique landscapes and breathtaking views of the Aegean Sea.

Evening

- Return to Kos and Final Dinner

After your return to Kos, wrap up your trip with a final dinner in Kos Town. Dine at a cozy restaurant near the Old Town, and celebrate your final evening with traditional meze platters, local wines, and perhaps a shot of rakomelo to toast your adventure.

This 3-day itinerary offers a perfect mix of culture, relaxation, and adventure on Kos Island. From the ancient ruins and charming villages to beautiful beaches and island-hopping excursions, your time on Kos will be filled with unforgettable experiences that showcase the island's diversity and beauty.

Conclusion

As you've discovered throughout this guide, Kos Island is a destination that offers something for every traveler. Whether you're drawn to its rich history, stunning beaches, vibrant culture, or outdoor adventures, Kos leaves an unforgettable impression with its blend of the ancient and the modern. From exploring the island's archaeological wonders to relaxing on pristine sands, every corner of Kos tells a story.

The island's charm extends beyond its historical landmarks and natural beauty. Its warm, welcoming people, lively festivals, and delicious local cuisine create a travel experience that is both authentic and immersive. Whether you're enjoying a peaceful sunset in Zia, hiking the lush trails of Mount Dikeos, or diving into the crystal-clear waters of the Aegean, Kos provides endless opportunities for discovery and relaxation.

As your journey to Kos comes to an end, we hope this guide has equipped you with everything you need to make your visit unforgettable. Kos is more than just a destination—it's a place where you can immerse yourself in history, indulge in adventure, and create lifelong memories. Whether this was your first visit or one of many, Kos will always be ready to welcome you back with open arms.

Printed in Great Britain
by Amazon